Praise for *The Thinking Effect*

"In *The Thinking Effect*, Mike Vaughan provides great insight into why most training programs fail, and more importantly, what to do about it. The book is transformational, thoughtful, and provocative. Mike provides a vision and path for the future and calls us to rethink thinking. He succinctly lays out 'how to use cutting-edge simulations to engage individuals in a virtuous cycle that involves improving thinking, applying it to different situations, and learning from the outcome—a cycle that changes mental models and reveals what we call the Thinking Effect.' A must read—I believe that this will become one of the most important books in our field!"

—Chris Hardy, Ph.D., Director, Global Learning and
Technology Center, Defense Acquisition University

"Mike Vaughan has nailed a critical leadership and learning issue and the way out of it. His book should be a 'must read' for individuals and organizations that want to make a difference."

—Vice Admiral Richard H. Truly,
US Navy, Ret. NASA Astronaut TO

"Finally a book that articulates a simple methodology of how to think versus what to think, that is sustainable, scalable, agnostic to time, economy, politics, and social and cultural bias. As I read through the book, the very activities getting in my way of thinking were happening as if he was narrating those very moments. Great leaders are not perfect, they succeed and fail. Failing forward, assimilating, adapting, and applying the lessons learned is the differentiator this author so artfully describes."

—Rodahl Leong-Lyons,
Vice President of Sales—Americas, HYATT

"The way the world does business has changed dramatically in the last decade and it will continue to change. That means education—especially education for professionals and higher education—must continue to change, continue to rethink aspects of their value propositions. Michael Vaughan is ahead of the curve in mapping how critical thinking and imagination are re-emerging as essentials for leadership in all fields."

—John P. Fitzgibbons, S.J., President, Regis University

"The noisy debates about whether schools are failing or work-force skills are slipping skips over the fundamental question, 'What is it we want our graduates and employees to know?' *The Thinking Effect* argues persuasively that they should learn how to think. The lessons it offers, from cognitive science and neuro-biology, provide a clear guide as to how training and education can best achieve that goal."

—Peter Cappelli, George W. Taylor Professor of Management, The University of Pennsylvania Wharton School, author of *Talent on Demand*

THE
THINKING EFFECT

RETHINKING THINKING
to Create GREAT LEADERS
and the NEW VALUE WORKER

MICHAEL VAUGHAN

NICHOLAS BREALEY
PUBLISHING

BOSTON · LONDON

First published in the United States of America and
Great Britain by Nicholas Brealey Publishing in 2013

20 Park Plaza, Suite 610
Boston, MA 02116 USA
Tel: + 617-523-3801
Fax: + 617-523-3708

3-5 Spafield Street, Clerkenwell
London, EC1R 4QB, UK
Tel: +44-(0)-207-239-0360
Fax: +44-(0)-207-239-0370

www.nicholasbrealey.com
www.thethinkingeffect.com

© 2013 by Michael Vaughan
Graphic images by Julie Leidel
Product images by Chris Kline

Cover Design: Laura Manthey Design

Printed in the United States of America
18 17 16 15 14 13 1 2 3 4 5 6 7 8 9 10

ISBN: 978-1-85788-599-6
E-ISBN: 978-1-85788-933-8

Library of Congress Cataloging-in-Publication Data
Vaughan, Michael, 1970–
    The thinking effect : rethinking thinking to create great leaders and the new value worker / by Michael Vaughan.
        pages cm
    Includes bibliographical references.
    ISBN 978-1-85788-599-6 (pbk.) — ISBN 978-1-85788-933-8 (ebook)
    1. Organizational learning.   2. Organizational effectiveness.   3. Thought and thinking.   I. Title.
    HD58.82.V38 2013
    658.3'124—dc23

                                                                2013018714

Dedication

· ·

To my amazing wife, Stefania, and my children, Stan, Evan, and Nica: You are the greatest thinkers and leaders in my life. Your support, love, and encouragement made this book happen.

To my colleagues at The Regis Company: thank you for embracing the audacious vision of changing the way organizations learn.

Acknowledgments

....

This book, from its original concept to its final form, represents the synthesis of ideas and input from many people. Since the list is so vast, I can't insert all the names here—but you know who you are! I wholeheartedly want to thank each of you for your time, insights, and guidance. As you read these pages, I hope I represented your contributions thoughtfully.

I would like to offer a special thanks to Bill Husson and Regis University, in Denver, Colorado, for providing the resources to start The Regis Company. And to my research and editing team, Meredith Jones and Jenny Sullivan, for being great sounding boards and dealing with my endless revisions.

Several people have taken extra time over the past two decades to help guide my thinking, and this, in turn, has shaped who I am—both as a leader and as a person. The first person I would like to acknowledge is Ed Yoblonski. I met Ed in 1990 during my first college internship. After graduating from college in 1993, Ed hired me to lead a team of twenty-seven people who were responsible for monitoring the phone system across the Western United States. All the people on my team were members of a telecommunications union. On my first day on the job, Mary—a member of my team who also happened to be lead representative of the union—said to me, "I've been at this job more years than you are old, and I'm going to watch every move you make." And she did. I was written up for a union violation almost every week for the first few months. Through Ed's guidance, however, I learned the true essence of leadership. During the course of my first year, we created a fun and supportive team. In fact, Mary asked me if I would serve as the representative between the union and management during contract renegotiations that following summer.

The next individual who took me under his wing was Dr. Tony D'Souza, a Jesuit priest from India. After spending time in management positions at large organizations, I had become downhearted with the leaders around me. Many were close minded and old school, with no desire to change. In my pursuit of answers and insights, I met Tony at a retreat he was leading in Colorado. He taught me about limiting beliefs and helped me uncover my own. Shortly after the retreat, I tossed on a backpack and went to India to stay at various villages and retreat centers outside Mumbai that Tony organized for me. During that time I learned the importance of self-awareness and awareness of others.

I met Peggy Steele in 1995, when she acquired my first software company. Let's just say this world needs more leaders like Peggy. She could tell you that you screwed up in such a way that you would actually feel inspired to change. Peggy shaped my thinking about leadership and the importance of research. She challenged me to do, dream, and become more. Many of the ideas in this book were seeded by Peggy and her challenge to find new ways of educating others.

After reading Peter Senge's book, *The Fifth Discipline*, I was inspired but at the same time confused about how to actually implement the many revolutionary ideas he discussed. That's where Rod Walker, systems modeler par excellence, came in. Rod has helped evolve my thinking in the areas of system dynamics and systems and critical thinking.

I would like to thank Nicholas Brealey, Susannah, and the Nicholas Brealey Publishing team for their commitment and insightful guidance.

I would like to acknowledge my parents, Jim and Rose Vaughan. Words cannot describe my good fortune in having parents who are supportive of my dreams and choices.

Finally, I need to acknowledge all my colleagues at The Regis Company. Through their unrelenting pursuit of excellence at what they do, I have been able to witness what amazing systems thinkers and leaders can achieve.

Contents

Preface

....

> ... The methods that have been used in the past to
> develop leaders really, truly, categorically will not be
> enough for the complexity of challenges, which are on
> their way for organizations (and broader society).... The
> art of practicing this area well is going to get much harder,
> at the same time as it becomes much more important.
>
> —Nick Petrie, *Future Trends in Leadership Development*

FOR ORGANIZATIONS AND SOCIETIES to grow in a healthy and
sustainable way, people must learn *how to think* in novel and
emerging situations. In our increasingly interconnected and interdependent world, unique and complex situations emerge daily.
The hard truth is that old patterns of thought will no longer suf-
fice; to remain competitive, organizations must rethink thinking.

I've been working in this area—driving new ways of thinking
by creating new ways of learning—for more than 20 years. My
background is in cognitive and computer science. I originally
set out to teach computers to think, a field called artificial intelligence (AI). The field of AI aims to study and design intelligent
technology: think *Terminator*. My particular area of interest is
in a subfield called artificial neural networks, which attempts

to model how the human brain learns through repetition and reinforcement. Similar to how our brains work, an artificial neural network learns from experience, not from programming. For example, I was able to teach a dot matrix printer—the kind that had the printer head mounted on a rod—to balance a pole much like people balance poles in the palms of their hands. We mounted a pole to the printer head, and any time the pole fell left or right, the neural network controlling the printer head received negative feedback. When it was able to keep the pole upright, it received positive reinforcement. In time, the neural network learned to balance a pole. Cool, right?

Yet even with these advances, at the time I studied this technology, I realized that computing power and the practical application of artificial neural networks was limited. Consequently, I set out on a journey to find a convergence of the things that I'm extremely passionate about: neuroscience, learning, and technology. During my research, I came across a book by Peter Senge titled *The Fifth Discipline: The Art and Practice of the Learning Organization*. His book truly shaped my thinking, and it certainly influenced many of the ideas and concepts in this book. I must admit, however, that it has taken me almost a decade to truly understand the depth of the ideas outlined in Senge's book. Since my first reading of *The Fifth Discipline*, I set a goal to make its concepts more accessible to organizations. At the time, I had a gut feeling that if people could truly develop their minds to see and understand the world as a system, then individual and organizational performance would be more effective and purposeful.

I needed more than a gut feeling, however, and equally important, I needed to find ways to help people learn and apply this new way of thinking.

My search took me deeper into neuroscience, behavioral science, educational science, and computer science. I started in neuroscience by researching the brain's ability to adapt its structural and functional organization. This area of study is called *neuroplasticity*, and it has guided my thinking on how to create the conditions necessary for workers to generate their own insights. Behavioral science shined a light on the common internal barriers, including fear of failure, that limit us. This research took me to India, where I spent considerable time with Jesuits who had developed techniques for exposing and rewriting our limiting beliefs.

I studied the science of education because I wanted to understand why most training is ineffective and why organizations keep repeating the same mistakes year after year. Finally, my colleagues and I created an essential breakthrough in computer technology that allows us to pull all these ideas together into a scalable, cost-effective environment to provide global organizations with solutions that focus on this new way of thinking.

In 2003, I joined The Regis Company, a talented and determined group of people at the forefront of custom simulation design. They have made it their life's journey to identify new ways of thinking that are driven by new ways of learning.

This book shares what my colleagues and I have learned about creating great leaders and value workers by igniting in individuals the ability to think and generate enduring value. I share how we use cutting-edge simulations to engage individuals in a virtuous cycle that involves improving thinking, applying it to different situations, and learning from the outcome—a cycle that changes mental models and reveals what we call "the Thinking Effect."

The Thinking Effect is both an individual experience and a collective process an organization can jumpstart for its employees. The most powerful aspect of the Thinking Effect is that everyone can learn to participate in it. Let's find out more.

Introduction

M ORE THAN FIFTY YEARS AGO, author Kurt Vonnegut published a short story called "Harrison Bergeron," which was set in a future world that mandated all people be equal in talent, intelligence, and appearance. Those who were considered average remained as they were, but those who had any exceptional abilities were forced to wear handicaps to ensure they did not surpass the average. Beautiful people wore masks, and the strong carried heavy weights.

The most intriguing handicap, however, was for those who were deemed intelligent. Those individuals wore radio earpieces that blasted a tremendous noise every few minutes. The noise was intended to distract them so they would not be able to maintain exceptional thought processes or develop ideas. This would ensure that they remained average.

Sound like a familiar problem? Vonnegut's fiction seems eerily relevant today.

A team at the University of California at Irvine tracked, minute by minute, how individuals spend their time during a workday. They found that the average employee could spend only 11 minutes on a project before she encountered an interruption such as an e-mail, phone call, or knock on the door. Rebounding from the interruption took an average of twenty-five minutes, if the employee returned to the original task at all.[1] With numbers like these, the odds of quality thinking and decision making occurring—or even any work happening at all, it would seem—are stacked against us.

Like Vonnegut's characters, we are all subjected to a steady stream of thought-stopping distractions. And in the same way, the result is often subpar output and average work, even from the most exceptional individuals and prestigious organizations.

One notable difference between Vonnegut's fictional world and the world in which we live is that organizations do not want employees to remain average. Yet, most business training is only average.

Businesses are dynamic, complex systems, and to understand them requires a new way of thinking. Employees at all levels must think differently about their jobs, the organization, and the markets they serve. This type of thinking does not come from slogans or from internal communications or from traditional training. This new type of thinking develops through a virtuous cycle of learning, trying, reflecting, and trying again. It is the type of thinking that helps individuals to understand cause and effect, short- and long-term delay results, unintended consequences, and interdependencies of the system within which they work. This form of thinking has become essential to an organization's—and an individual's—enduring value.

Most employees, no matter how smart and capable, do not grasp the complex interdependencies at work in their organization. This is not due to the lack of communications, process flows, or training. This lack of understanding happens because

---

[1] Gloria Mark, Victor M. Gonzalez, and Justin Harris, "No Task Left Behind? Examining the Nature of Fragmented Work," *Proceedings of the 2005 Conference on Human Factors in Computing Systems* (CHI 2005, Portland, Oregon, April 2–7, 2005): 321–30.

we all live and work in a world that is changing quickly and is often difficult for us to get our heads around. This complexity has been the impetus of my research with colleagues at The Regis Company and the premise for this book.

In the pages that follow, I share our team's journey from understanding what it takes to be valuable in a volatile, uncertain, complex, and ambiguous business world to developing new technologies and methodologies that create enduring value for clients. I explain why—whether you are a manager, leader, consultant, or just a thinking person within an organization—you benefit by moving from the linear approach of telling employees *what to think* to systemic learning, in which employees learn *how to think*.

Through real-life insights, cases, and original research, this book explores the challenges and best practices for developing the skills and abilities of all employees. This information is crucial to leadership today if businesses seek to build the type of organization that promulgates growth, understanding, and improvement for clients and employees alike.

Ultimately, the book highlights the Thinking Effect and the power it has to sustain individuals to the point where their value spans beyond the boundaries of the organization. This new way of thinking will improve decision making and collaboration, affecting the ability of individuals and organizations to solve problems and generate value.

The medium for creating leaders and organizations that embrace a new way of thinking is the simulation. Unlike traditional business training, which focuses on the transmission of knowledge and information, this technology incorporates the tools necessary for teams to collaborate in solving complex problems and generating monumental insights. Simulations enable participants to engage in (and with) action, feedback, and reflection in a variety of contextually relevant scenarios.

Simulations enable managers, leaders, and consultants to help employees develop the patterns of thought that differentiate top performers from those who merely do their jobs. At The Regis Company we also use simulations to help people identify new techniques for refining mental models and to help them embrace the practices for improving decision making and collaboration—all of which affect an individual's and an organization's ability to solve problems and generate enduring value. These techniques and practices serve as the heart of the pages that follow.

NEURAL LEADERSHIP

Throughout this book, I present insights into the psychology of individuals at work by leveraging the latest research from neuroscience plus practical experience from our leadership programs. These brief descriptions are meant for reflection. I hope they will stimulate your interest in exploring the needs of the brains that power both workers and organizations. These insights are also intended to inspire you to develop your "neural leadership" to help meet the psychological needs of individuals and to enable the Thinking Effect.

PART I
....

What to Think versus How to Think

THE IMPACT OF POOR THINKING is not a challenge reserved for a few struggling companies; it is a challenge faced by individuals and organizations globally.

The Millennium Project is an undertaking that began in 1996 with the goal to create a global collective intelligence system to improve prospects for the future of humanity. There are now forty countries taking part in the project, each represented by think-tank futurists, scholars, business planners, and policy makers who work for international organizations, governments, corporations, nongovernment organizations, and universities. Every year, the Millennium Project releases an annual *State of the Future* report. The report discusses 15 Global Challenges and includes the model shown in Figure 1, which serves as a framework for assessing the global and local prospects for humanity.[1] Take a look at the fifteen challenges on this image—there is one that just does not seem to fit with the rest.

---

[1] The Millennium Project, "15 Global Challenges Facing Humanity," last modified 2009, www.millennium-project.org/millennium/challeng.html.

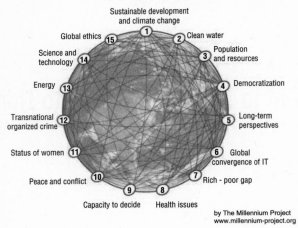

FIGURE 1 15 Global Challenges
(Reprinted with permission)

It is interesting that "Capacity to decide"—that is, decision making—finds a place on the same list of global challenges as clean water, peace and conflict, and energy. Why does decision making rank on this list? The report explains that due to increasing complexity, proliferation of data, and global interdependency, the lack of quality decision making is becoming a systemic problem.

> We have far more data, evidence, and computer models to make decisions today, but that also means we have far more information overload and excessive choice proliferation. The number and complexity of choices seem to be growing beyond our abilities to analyze, synthesize, and make decisions. The acceleration of change reduces the time from recognition of the need to make a decision to completion of all the steps to make the right

decision. . . . *Many of the world's decision making processes*
are inefficient, slow, and ill informed. [emphasis added]

—*The Millennium Project, State of the Future*[2]

That highlighted sentence emphasizes the core of this global problem. The consequence of an increasingly complex world is that people are being challenged in new ways to make quality decisions, based on quality thinking, that affect their lives and the lives of those with whom they interact. Complexity defines the interconnected and interdependent relationships that form an organization. It explains how one decision in one division can inadvertently affect another division. It provides insight into why people are so stressed, why it is hard to hold people accountable, why it is difficult to get things done, and why change is difficult.

Compounding the issue of complexity is the endless noise of incomplete and conflicting information. I'm not just talking about the ringing of phones and chiming of electronic conversations, though these too affect our ability to focus. I'm talking about noise as "an unwanted signal or disturbance; irrelevant or meaningless data occurring along with desired information."[3] In our personal and work lives, *noise* has become the word used to describe the constant barrage of information and distractions that obscure our judgment and reduce our ability to think and communicate clearly. We feel its effect when we go to the supermarket and are presented with too many options, when we receive an onslaught of e-mails and reports, or when we are fed thirty-second messages telling us *what to think*.

---

[2] The Millennium Project, "15 Global Challenges Facing Humanity," last modified 2009, www.millennium-project.org/millennium/challeng.html.
[3] Merriam-Webster Online, s.v. "noise," www.merriam-webster.com/dictionary/noise.

At The Regis Company, we have observed the impacts that complexity and noise have on participants within our simulations. Over the past ten years, we've developed custom simulations for global organizations in a variety of topics, such as strategic alignment, leadership development, business and financial acumen, project management, talent management, customer service, product development, innovation, and the list goes on. Regardless of the industry or an individual's level within the organization, we have found four consistent themes:

1. Most employees are poor decision makers.
2. When problems become complex, most people fall back to surface-level thinking.
3. Most individuals know how to communicate well but are poor at collaborating when confronted with unique situations.
4. When the amount of noise is increased, individual effectiveness further decreases.

Despite the large amount of money organizations spend on training, these themes render the training ineffective, which bewilders training departments and executives alike. Why, then, with so many resources invested in addressing these issues, has there been little improvement in the way we make decisions, solve problems, or collaborate?

The reason, as Albert Einstein is said to have pointed out, is, "We cannot solve our problems with the same thinking we used when we created them." Most people still learn to think in a linear fashion and continue with this technique throughout their lives. Yet if organizations hope to remedy situations that were created by linear thinking, then they must encourage workers to approach these issues with a different mindset.

In their book *The Knowing-Doing Gap: How Smart Companies Turn Knowledge into Action*, Jeffrey Pfeffer and Robert I.

Sutton point out that most people *know* more than they actually *do*.[4] For example, people tend to know far more about healthy eating and exercising than they put into practice. The authors relate that many organizations provide forty or more hours of training per year for each employee, yet many workers still lack the ability to do much outside of what they have been told. Accomplishments are often the result of a heroic effort from twenty percent of the employees, while the other eighty percent merely do enough to get by. Why is there such a huge gap? The gap is created because the *what-to-think* educational model prepares individuals to function primarily inside known and predictable situations—an important skill, but not enough. This approach produces a large number of linear thinkers throughout the world and provides insight into why more and more employees are ineffective in an increasingly complex world.

NEURAL LEADERSHIP

Understanding the need for security

Your organization is unique, with many processes, policies, strategies, goals, issues, and daily challenges. To improve the overall performance of the organization in the long term, employee behavior needs to continually change—an issue that proves difficult for many. The US Army War College (AWC) defines a practical code for leaders in a complex world, which they call VUCA:

- **V**olatility describes the nature, dynamics, and speed of change.
- **U**ncertainty refers to the lack of predictability and understanding of issues and events.

---

[4] Jeffrey Pfeffer and Robert I. Sutton, *The Knowing-Doing Gap: How Smart Companies Turn Knowledge into Action* (Boston, MA: Harvard Business School Press, 2000).

- **C**omplexity defines the forces that surround an organization.
- **A**mbiguity addresses the potential for misreads, mixed meanings, and cause-and-effect confusion.

  From a brain perspective, any one of these states may create insecurity in the minds of employees. Lacking time to process things that change too quickly, not being able to thoughtfully predict an event due to its complexity, or dealing with potentially making a mistake because of conflicting or incomplete information—all of these things can pose a threat to the brain.

  The solution is a rather simple formula: Leaders must help people move beyond their fear to a place of security. If people feel threatened, and if this feeling leads to fear, then their performance will decrease. If people feel threatened but are encouraged and supported to move beyond that fear to achieve a sense of security, then they will be more likely to stay engaged and find solutions. Understanding this innate need for the brain to feel security will help you help others.

Why Do We Focus on What to Think?

Most training models and technologies are based on the premise that knowledge is power. Training focuses on transmitting information from teacher to student with the idea that the mere accumulation of knowledge will equip the student to function effectively in the world. "Sage-on-the-stage" workshops and basic e-learning courses reinforce a model built around filling students' minds with information. However, a closer look at how the brain is wired, how adults learn, and what creates sustainable change reveals that the mainstream models are missing the mark.

Traditional training programs are designed to improve performance in a specific area of practice. Traditionally, students go to history class to memorize dates, people, and events. In math, they memorize rules and theorems. To become accountants, students accumulate a vast amount of information during the course of school. When they enter the workforce, this foundation is expanded through specific training in organizational rules, processes, regulations, and industry-specific financial terms.

There are more than fifty different methodologies for designing training programs and interventions. Though the steps, tools, and duration of the methodologies vary, most produce training that focuses on the bottom three levels of Bloom's Taxonomy[5]: knowledge, comprehension, and application. Knowledge defines an individual's ability to recall data (e.g., reciting a definition of a term). Comprehension means the individual can take the definition and restate it using his own words. Achieving the Application level means the individual can apply the definition to a task. The next three levels—synthesis, evaluation, and creation—refer to his ability to draw correlations from disparate data points, assess outcomes as a result of some decision or action, and develop new courses of action, respectively. The bottom three levels can be equated to teaching people *what to think*. The top three levels are focused on teaching people *how to think*.

At The Regis Company, we have developed the Learning Impact Tool shown in Figure 2 to categorize the different types of training solutions in relation to their Richness and Reach. *Richness* is defined as the impact of the learning. Along the Richness axis, you will see the levels of Bloom's Taxonomy (knowledge, comprehension, application, analysis, synthesis, evaluation, and creation). The higher on the Richness axis a solution falls, the greater the depth of learning. The *Reach* axis describes the number of people who participate in the training. The further to the right a solution falls, the greater the number of participants.

---

[5] Benjamin Bloom, *Taxonomy of Educational Objectives* (Boston, MA: Allyn and Bacon, 1956).

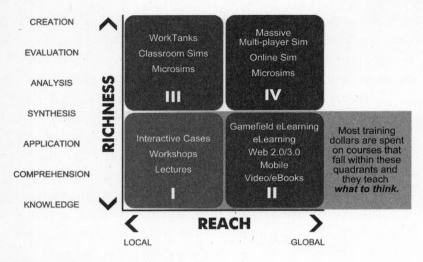

FIGURE 2 Learning Impact Tool

Quadrant I, in the lower left, depicts learning solutions with relatively low levels of richness (focused almost exclusively on information that the student needs to know) and limited reach. Workshops, even those that incorporate role-plays or activities, fall in the spectrum of Quadrant I.

Quadrant II, in the lower right corner, shows solutions that build a foundation of knowledge through online media—thus reaching a larger number of employees. E-learning and various social media/Web 2.0/3.0 options make up this quadrant.

These *what-to-think* quadrants focus on providing employees with knowledge and comprehension. Courses might help them recall data and information, or learn facts, processes, and procedures.

The *how-to-think* quadrants, III and IV, focus on the higher cognitive skills, such as analysis, synthesis, evaluation, and creation. As Bloom wisely pointed out, the higher-order thinking skills are personally and organizationally more valuable in the long term, because they can be applied in a variety of situations and they prepare the learner for unexpected variations.

Quadrant III, in the upper left corner, represents learning solutions with relatively high levels of richness (experiences that challenge us to learn *how to think*) but limited reach, such as classroom-based simulations or WorkTanks. A WorkTank combines learning with the actual production of a needed work product for the organization. For example, within a strategic alignment WorkTank, participants develop actual strategies and vet them by running various scenarios across different market conditions.

A Quadrant III microsim generally is a shorter simulation that focuses on a few skills. It is often included in classroom activities or embedded within e-learning modules to increase the richness and provide skill practices.

Quadrant IV, in the upper right corner, represents solutions that provide high levels of richness *and* reach through online technologies, such as massive, multiple-player simulations. Quadrant IV–type massive, multiplayer simulations are targeted at global organizations requiring deep learning and global reach. These simulations incorporate the tools necessary for teams to collaborate in solving complex problems.

While Quadrants III and IV offer more effective *how-to-think* learning experiences, most of today's training falls into Quadrants I and II. The impact of these programs is often measured by collecting "smile sheets" or "seat time." The number of people touched is a primary measure of success for this type of learning—there is plenty of content, but actual behavioral impact is minimal.

I learned the inefficiency of these types of solutions the hard way in 2000. I was the vice president of a training company that was flush with cash, had seasoned leaders, created a well-defined strategy, and employed talented people with energy and ideas. If a problem arose, we solved it quickly. If plans needed to be made, we sat in lengthy meetings and captured Specific, Measurable, Achievable, Realistic, and Time-bound (SMART) objectives. We readily made decisions—a lot of them. But we eventually discovered that we were highly ineffective. The problems we solved often arose again with greater fortitude. We thought we had clear communication processes, but we certainly did not understand how to collaborate to satisfy our SMART objectives. Most of the decisions we made were either self-serving or detrimental to another part of our business; we were not thinking systemically.

The icing on the cake was that we were teaching decision making, problem solving, and other leadership skills to our clients in our award-winning e-learning modules and workshops. These solutions, however, were all in Quadrants I and II. We did not equip our employees or our clients to adapt to new situations, to develop a systemic view, or to collaborate across divisions to solve the organization's most pressing needs. We simply taught them to work within known situations. The business shut down within a few years—it was a humbling and eye-opening experience. Despite the fact that our approaches to learning had caught the eye of some learning gurus because the solutions used the latest technology, we were still teaching people *what to think*. This experience shaped me personally, and it gave me great insight into why most training does little more than prepare employees to function within known situations.

DEEPLY ROOTED HISTORY

The evolution of current teaching methods began with the best of intentions. For centuries, education was shaped by great thinkers such as Socrates, who understood the power of dialogue, reflection, and fostering an environment in which students generated their own insights. This was a rich type of learning. Deep questioning led to deep reflection, which in turn allowed for self-generated insights. However, this type of learning could reach only a select few pupils at once, and it took time. What this approach had in richness, it lacked in reach.

The history of public education in the United States is a perfect example of reach. Today's learning practices can be traced to the work of Horace Mann, who was secretary of the Massachusetts State Board of Education and, in 1848, was elected to the US House of Representatives. Mann was a vocal advocate for universal public education as the best way to both "equalize the condition of men" and turn the nation's "unruly" children into disciplined, judicious citizens. He created the Normal School, which established standards and norms for training high school graduates to be teachers.

Following the example of Massachusetts, other states began to adopt the Prussian education system that Mann favored. This system consisted of a standardized curriculum for each grade level and widespread testing, which was used to classify children for potential career training. This approach to education was beneficial during the Industrial Age as the population exploded.

The Industrial Age was a major turning point in history. Many countries experienced unprecedented growth due to automation, new production methods, new iron manufacturing processes, and more efficient power generation. These revolutionary improvements required many new workers, who needed new skills. This need was met by the establishment of an education system designed to reach the masses. Standards and methods were created, and many of them still exist today. But the effort to broaden the reach to more people quickly diluted the quality of the experience.

Author and educator Oliver Van DeMille calls this standardized education system a ". . . conveyor belt education . . .

which tries to prepare everyone for a job, any job, by teaching them *what* to think. This includes rudimentary skills to help them function in society."[6]

You needn't look much further than the majority of primary schools to see Van DeMille's conveyor belt analogy in action. Students are exposed to vast amounts of information and foundational skills. Along the way, quality checkpoints verify that students learn the information deemed "appropriate." The conveyor belt carries them into middle school, where they learn logic, basic concepts, and theories. They move on to high school and are introduced to rhetoric, and a select few are given a chance to learn additional advanced concepts. The conveyor belt drops students off at a university, where they are further shaped by career-specific information. In theory, as the assembled widget tumbles from the conveyor belt and into the shipping basket that is society, we are left to believe that these students are now prepared to think and act in the situations and conditions life will throw at them.

The "conveyor belt" system of education trains children in what they need to do to get by in the role of a typical knowledge worker: repeat information, read assigned chapters, print clearly in the box, and do not speak unless called upon. Students are not encouraged to let their questions wander; subjects are segregated, few connections are made between courses, and their ability to think systemically is dulled.

As our world has drastically evolved over recent years, many school systems have begun to incorporate different learning tools and styles into the typical classroom. Old habits are difficult to change, however, and though we know that everything is connected to everything else, we still tend to box subjects into

---

[6] Oliver Van DeMille, *A Thomas Jefferson Education: Teaching a Generation of Leaders for the Twenty-first Century* (Cedar City, UT: George Wythe College Press, 2002), 21.

topics and competencies and neglect the underlying dynamics that connect it all. Unfortunately, understanding these systems is where deep learning occurs, where students gain the abilities to become valuable workers. The world demands valuable workers, but we are still teaching our children to be knowledge workers.

The seduction of the current educational system is the notion of identifying *measurable results*. We produce tests to measure "performance," to sedate anxious parents, and to fuel unnecessary policy. Amazing educators, who pour their hearts and minds into shaping our youth, often find themselves limited by this antiquated approach to education. Given the sheer number of children enrolled in schools and the overwhelming amount of information available to them, an emphasis on testing is understandable. But too often, test taking becomes a practice in rote memorization instead of an experiment in processing information and reasoning that leads to self-generated insights.

Unfortunately, education does not improve greatly at the university level. Richard Arum, professor of Sociology and Education at New York University, captured research regarding how very little students are actually learning. In his book *Academically Adrift: Limited Learning on College Campuses*, he finds that 45 percent of the United States' college attendees show no gains in knowledge during their first two years in college. Furthermore, 36 percent showed little change in knowledge after four years. The report showed that students spend 50 percent less time studying today than they did in the 1980s. There is no need to put in more time, as they are being taught to the test. Equally alarming, even with this half-hearted approach, the students in the report maintain a 3.2 grade point average.[7]

---

[7] Richard Arum and Josipa Roksa, *Academically Adrift: Limited Learning on College Campuses* (Chicago: University of Chicago Press, 2011).

The business world has done little to improve the efficacy of learning. Every year, there is a new "how-to" book or a trending program guaranteed to get results. Many companies have jumped aboard the technology train, overlaying the latest Web 2.0/3.0 platforms, apps, and dashboards because "flashy" has become synonymous with "effective." However, many of these programs offer little more than new delivery platforms and engagement tricks—as if delivering a greasy burger on a silver platter makes it any more palatable or nutritious than presentation in a paper wrapper.

So, let's go ahead and throw all *what-to-think* training out the window and be done with it, right? Of course not!

Organizations need to continue to selectively invest in foundational knowledge because it is the mental mortar that fills knowledge gaps. As people learn more and do more, there are *always* knowledge gaps that need to be bridged. *What-to-think* training has a real purpose. It provides consistency and a common way of thinking. Understanding processes, methodologies, and the organizational "way" is imperative for preparing employees.

I'm not prepared to disassemble the conveyor belt quite yet. Public and professional educational systems do what they are designed to do by producing a relatively literate and productive workforce.

As mentioned at the beginning of this section, there are other practical abilities and skills that are necessary for workers to function effectively. These include job-specific skills—such as customer service, accounting, or computer programming—or traditional leadership skills—such as business acumen, innovation, or strategic planning. Most organizations have made these traditional skills their primary focus.

While these skills are important and must continue to be part of an organization's curriculum, managers, leaders, and consultants must accept that value-driven learning requires more than the knowledge of tools and processes and a firm backbone. Procedures are only as good as the people who understand how to leverage them in unique situations.

In a changing world, there are no guarantees that specific knowledge will remain relevant. In these levels of learning focused on knowledge and comprehension, workers are not equipped with the thinking abilities to understand the broader context or changing realities in which they may find themselves. The result is overwhelmed and overworked employees.

No matter how much traditional training organizations put into workers, the extent to which they can add value depends on how well they can unlearn old patterns of thought and replace them with new patterns. Let's face it: It's an increasingly complex world, and memorizing eight concepts will not be as important as being able to quickly learn and do two new tasks. Organizations need people who can *do* more—and do it with speed and thoughtfulness.

Why We Need to Focus on How to Think

"Failure does not strike like a bolt from the blue," points out Dietrich Dörner, emeritus professor of General and Theoretical Psychology at Otto-Friedrich University in Bamberg, Germany, and recipient of the Gottfried Wilhelm Leibniz Prize (the highest honor awarded in German research). He goes on to share his insight: ". . . complicated situations seem to elicit habits of thought that set failure in motion from the beginning. From that point, the continuing complexity of the task and the growing apprehension of failure encourage methods of decision making that make failure even more likely and then inevitable."[8]

---

[8] Dietrich Dörner, *The Logic of Failure: Recognizing and Avoiding Error in Complex Situations* (New York: Metropolitan Books, 1996), 10.

Our brains have been trained to adeptly handle straight-forward situations. Learning has focused on linear, cause-and-effect scenarios and isolated decision-making tasks. With our learning radar focusing on *what to think*, we are unprepared to act amid complexity. We are setting these patterns of thought into motion, and it is virtually inevitable that habitual thinking will lead to failure in the complexity of today's world.

COMPLEXITY

"Events, threats and opportunities aren't just coming at us faster or with less predictability," says IBM Corporation CEO Samuel Palmisano in the introduction to "Capitalizing on Complexity," the company's fourth sweeping survey of CEOs. "They are converging and influencing each other to create entirely unique situations." IBM researchers conducted face-to-face conversations with more than 1,500 CEOs from around the world. Their analysis of the interviews identified three themes:

- A rapid escalation of *complexity* is the biggest challenge confronting both public- and private-sector organizations today.

- Less than half of those interviewed feel that their enterprises are equipped to cope effectively with this complexity.

- The single most important leadership competency for enterprises seeking a path through this complexity is *creativity.*[9]

Clearly, the problem of complexity has recently claimed a spot in the forefront of the business landscape. The truth is, however, that the problem of dealing with complexity is not some

---

[9] "Capitalizing on Complexity: Insights from the Global Chief Executive Officer Study," IBM Global Business Services (Somers, NY, 2010), 6.

new quest of the tech-savvy twenty-first century. Aspects of this complexity have always been apparent, though they have taken varying forms. In the 1920s, through advancements in quantum physics, people clearly saw the interconnectedness of the world. At that point, scientists uncovered that multiple particles are linked together in such a way that the measurement of one particle's quantum state determines the possible quantum states of the other particles. The world was complex even then, but the details of quantum physics did not intrude on most people's days.

As it is, we are optimized, task-driven thinkers. Even when numerous variables are introduced or vast amounts of information must be processed, we can usually follow cause-and-effect events (A caused B caused C, and so on). But going deeper requires that we suspend judgment and maintain both past and future in our exploration. At first, this can be a difficult concept to grasp because most of us have learned to think primarily in the here and now. We live in an event-oriented world in which 24/7 news is bombarding us with happenings from around the world, so we cannot be expected to respond any other way. Much of the information we receive is superficial or single-use and lacks underlying system data.

Information gathered at the superficial level may create a feeling of excitement and even confidence, but it rarely leads to sustainable solutions. This concept works nicely with—and results partly from—our linear thinking tendencies. Push the gas pedal, and the car goes faster. Press the brake, and the car slows. On the surface level, these seem straightforward, but even these examples may lead to nonlinearities. Push the gas pedal, and the car goes faster—until you get a ticket or run out of gas. Ride the brakes all the way down Mount Evans, and the brakes overheat and the car speeds up. Things that act linearly are frequently only linear over a certain limited range and over a certain period of time. Applying this level of thinking to scenarios that do not operate in a linear manner gets us into trouble.

Complexity means the existence of many interdependent elements in a system. When we think of an organization, we typically see a picture of the traditional hierarchy structure. There is a top that branches into groups that further branch into more groups and so on. The reality, however, of how an organization actually works and accomplishes tasks is a bit less neat. Figure 3, a model of a manufacturing organization, presents a high-level view of a more realistic organizational map.

In practice, there are actually many more interconnected elements that dynamically interact, shaping the behavior of the organization. But even from this simplified model, you can see the complexities of an organization and better understand

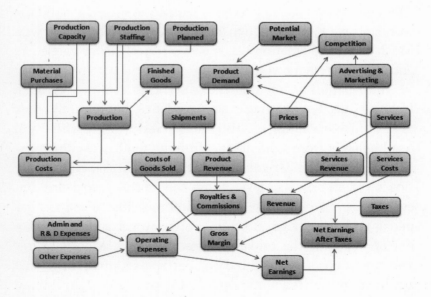

FIGURE 3 Model of a Manufacturing Organization

why decision making, problem solving, and collaboration are so difficult.

These are all concepts included in the field of system dynamics and systems thinking. System dynamics is an approach to understanding the behavior of complex systems by taking into consideration interconnected parts, feedback loops, and delays. Jay Forrester, a professor at the Massachusetts Institute of Technology, created the field of system dynamics in the 1950s after realizing the limitations of our linear thinking.

Top minds in the field of learning and system dynamics—such as John Sterman (1993), Dietrich Dörner (1996), Peter Senge (1995), Jay Forrester (1972), and Peter Drucker (1967)—all describe a variety of thinking patterns that frequently lead to poor or catastrophic decisions. Here are examples of how an individual's lack of higher-order thinking results in diminished decision performance:

- Failure to consider the entire system and its context.
- Failure to understand and accommodate the delayed effects of any proposed intervention.
- A narrow focus on the current problems without regard to future consequences.
- Failure to notice what is actually working in any given situation.

At The Regis Company, we have observed these patterns of thought and their negative effects in our simulations. Within the simulations, decision makers often try to solve one problem at a time, creating new problems in their wake. They tend to focus on the problems they have, ignoring problems that have not yet surfaced. As they become overloaded with information, they become even more fixated on the elements they think they can control.

COMPLEXITY: A CASE STUDY

While I was writing this book, I received an early morning call from a colleague, Beth, the COO of a large corporation, whose situation exemplified the complex issues companies are facing today. "Mike, this is what's going on. We went through some difficult layoffs. We're now facing competition from small businesses—some of which are halfway around the world. Our products are dated, and we're slow to adapt. The services we provide are in need of much improvement. We need to transform our company and our business. Let's talk."

Beth asked me to join her team for a meeting that evening in Washington, D.C., to discuss what it would take to transform her organization into the competitive and respected organization it was once known to be. Fortunately, I had a suitcase already packed from a recent trip, so I jumped in the car and drove to the airport to catch the next flight.

Our team had worked with this company before and knew all too well the headwinds that they were confronting. Merely suggesting they optimize their processes and tools, examine their competition, or explore new markets or acquisitions would be insulting. What Beth was asking for is far more important— and a bit less tangible. As I worked with Beth to create a new plan for the corporation, I shared many of the insights that will appear throughout the rest of this book. For now, let's take a quick look at the conventional approach that led them into trouble in the first place.

Beth's organization is global, with operations throughout the Americas, Europe, and Asia. The corporation faced relentless competition domestically, as well as fluctuations in unstable European markets. Despite these facts, the initial team was highly optimistic of their continued growth in the Asian markets, specifically in China. They decided to expand in select global markets where they believed their products and services would be greatly used. The plan was to first get into the market by investing as little as possible from existing US-based production lines. Products would be created, shipped, and sold locally in outlet stores throughout Beijing—a method of expansion similar to their European strategy just two years earlier. Beth had given her approval.

Six months into the plan, sales were up, margins were a bit below expectations, and demand looked promising. This wasn't much of a surprise. The pre-market research indicated that a substantial share of the market was open for the grabbing.

Beth was soon caught up in both the hype and the stress of the situation. News reports from all over the world were talking about stalled or collapsing economies. A new breed of competitors was entering the market. Economies in the surrounding regions were slowing. World noise was overflowing. Still, at breathtaking speeds, her team generated reports that thoughtfully confirmed their actions. They released memos, analyzed charts, and cataloged endless information. Consistent meetings caught all team members up on details, and checkpoints ensured everything was on time. Organizational noise greeted them at every corner. Before they knew it, they had buried themselves so deep in data and reports that finding any insightful patterns was next to impossible.

In Beth's situation, visible issues started to surface about nine months into the initiative. In hindsight, she realized the issues were there much earlier, but she and her team had neglected to notice the larger issue and instead had busied themselves with fixing small problems.

As the market response slowed and margins continued to get thinner, the team decided that they needed more data. They reassembled the research team and gave them a clear charter: gather new data, analyze it, determine what was going on, and fix it—quickly. The process took about a month, a very long month to the team that was watching their initiative corrode. After various contentious meetings, the team determined that the best course of action was to reinvest in earlier campaigns that generated the best results. To mitigate some of the risk, they also decided to ramp up manufacturing by shifting 30 percent of the production to their European facilities.

Rather than taking the time to *understand the underlying dynamics*, Beth's team reacted to issues as they surfaced, neglecting the fact that all the issues were somehow *interconnected*. We can laugh about it now, but when Beth was first describing her situation, it certainly was not funny. She said they were on a "crazy cycle." If sales went down, they would react by pushing marketing. When sales went up, they would react by pushing manufacturing, and when clients called upset, they would just react. Because they were always reacting, they did not have time to think or understand the dynamics.

Unfortunately, this is not an uncommon lesson. At The Regis Company, we see firsthand how often teams are derailed because they simply were not equipped to deal with the complexity. Developing an ability to understand the dynamics of systems has become critical to navigating the rampant complexity that greets us daily. Obviously, we can't control complexity. What we can control is our thinking—even in the face of some powerful factors that typically derail our thinking, such as biases, lack of attention, fear, too many choices, and a constant barrage of noise.

DERAILERS

Derailers are the primary reason why employees make poor decisions and erode collaboration between individuals and teams. The derailers can impact thinking to such an extreme that an individual's ability to learn, much less think, is rendered dull. The following is a brief overview about the main derailers we found participants exhibiting within our simulations when confronted with difficult and complex situations.

Bias

The brain is an incredible machine, continuously processing experiences to add to our understanding of our environment and prompting us to act based on these experiences. Sometimes, however, the models it constructs are flawed, and the brain itself contributes to the noise by seeking data to confirm a preconceived belief. This is referred to as *bias*. Human beings have a tendency to avoid information that might disprove our current ideas or throw our decision making into question. Instead, we seek—often without realizing it—answers that confirm our own biases. Bias is a type of internal noise that filters our experiences and affects the way we understand the world around us, allowing us to see what we want to see. It is a human tendency to draw a conclusion without considering the entire system or all of the evidence. As we gather information, our brains naturally reference memories and facts to interpret it based on what we already know. Often, the bias arises from one of three preformed sources:

- *Information processing shortcuts*, in which an individual makes an educated assumption, applying a general theory or overview rather than taking the time to fully review and consider information.
- *Social influences or beliefs*, which assume that something must be true because our belief system has taught us that it is.
- *Motivational factors*, which direct people to seek or consider primarily information that supports their existing ideas.

The information that employees *receive* is rarely entirely accurate, complete, and unbiased. The survey results on your desk, the report from your coworker, even the news on television—all of it has been filtered. Pieces may have been left out or distorted. Opinions may have influenced the conclusions.

There are many different types of biases, but these are the biases that my colleagues and I observed most often in our programs:

- *Confirmation bias* is one of the most detrimental to good decision making because it replaces deep thinking with consuming efforts to find information that will confirm a preconceived idea or theory. The project lead only seeks information that support his reasons for why the project is over budget.

- *Self-serving bias*, or the "it's not my fault" bias, focuses on placing the blame for failure elsewhere. It's amazing how when things get complicated, people act but do not want to take responsibility if the solution fails. When an initiative does not work, they find someone or something to blame. The account manager did not scope the project correctly! The leaders did not give me enough direction! If I only I had been allowed more time, I would have made a better decision.

- *Framing* is the process of selecting words that will encourage certain interpretations and discourage others. A situation can evoke different responses when presented using different words and context. For example, "global warming" versus "climate change" or "12 months" versus "1 year" or "you will lose" versus "you will gain" all evoke different emotions and thoughts. Framing is the most notorious culprit for causing world and organizational noise. It's effective because it pushes receivers of the message toward a preferred belief, giving people a mental shortcut to a conclusion. Politicians and leaders commonly use framing to package information in a certain way so it is more easily accepted by constituents.

- *Anchoring* occurs when someone relies too much on one piece of information and, as a result, places less importance on other data points.

- *Bandwagon effect* occurs when people do or believe the same thing because many others do or believe the same thing. I like to call this *social politeness bias*. In an effort to strive for consensus, we observed teams selecting not to properly appraise alternative courses of action. And when there is an executive on the team, everyone feels they should align with the business leader's view.

- *Information bias* is the tendency to seek information even when it cannot affect the outcome. With today's vast information resources, this is becoming more of a problem. When faced with fears of being wrong or organizational pressures such as downsizing, teams often seek information for the sake of it. The result is general busyness—but no significant movement forward.

- *Overconfidence* happens all too often when people overestimate their abilities. People may feel so certain about the validity of a certain piece of information or an action that they will follow through with it blindly—even though it's incorrect. Often, people who are confident about a plan tend to get approval over those who raise objections and point out risks. We see this behavior a lot in simulations. Participants do well in the first few rounds, become overly confident, and stop learning because they think they know better.

As you can imagine, if biases go unchecked, they may lead a highly talented and intelligent group of workers down the wrong path. There are also other types of derailers.

Attention

Attention made the derailer list because it has a direct impact on both learning and the effectiveness of quality thinking. A few years ago, the *New York Times* interviewed the 2005 MacArthur Fellowship ("Genius Grant") winners. When reporters asked the winners how they spent their daily commuting time, many said that they put their cell phones and iPods away, using the time instead for thinking without distraction.

The constant connectivity of the world and up-to-the-minute demands make it difficult for many of us to disconnect and engage in reflection. When was the last time you were able to separate from the world to think? How long has it been since you turned off e-mail at work to focus on one project? Or disconnected at home to reflect on your life? Our constant connection to technology can negatively affect our productivity and effectiveness. An information technology research firm in New York City found that interruptions now consume more than two hours of the average workday, or *28 percent* of our available time.[10] Is the answer, then, better multitasking? No!

Though employers say that the ability to multitask is one of the top characteristics they look for when interviewing candidates, studies support the theory that instead of adding to efficiency, juggling numerous projects and responsibilities actually steals company time and resources. When people try to multitask, they often create more problems by missing critical information or depleting mental resources. An individual's ability to provide valuable thought is diminished.

"Multi-tasking adversely affects how you learn," said Russell Poldrack, UCLA associate professor of Psychology and

---

[10] Clive Thompson, "Meet the Life Hackers," *The New York Times Magazine*, October 16, 2005, www.nytimes.com/2005/10/16/magazine/16guru.html.

coauthor of a 2006 study that examined participants' abilities while distracted. Poldrack's research also found the following:

> Even if you learn while multi-tasking, that learning is less flexible and more specialized, so you cannot retrieve the information as easily. Our study shows that to the degree you can learn while multi-tasking, you will use different brain systems. The best thing you can do to improve your memory is to pay attention to the things you want to remember.[11]

In another study, Teresa Amabile at Harvard Business School evaluated the daily work patterns of more than 9,000 individuals working on projects that required creativity and innovation under varying levels of time pressure. She and her colleagues confirmed that people are more creative when they focus on one activity for most of the day.[12]

Still not convinced you should turn off your e-mail while reading this book? Then here is another insightful study. Curious about how chronic multitaskers process information, researchers at Stanford University classified 262 university students as "heavy-media" or "low-media" multitaskers based on the number of media (television, music, computer games, phone calls, etc.) they consumed simultaneously. Based on the results of two questionnaires and three cognitive tests, the study concluded that heavy-media multitaskers were more likely to respond to stimuli outside their primary focus and have greater difficulty filtering irrelevant information. Surprisingly, chronic

---

[11] Russell Poldrack, "Multi-Tasking Adversely Affects the Brain's Learning Systems," UCLA Department of Psychology, July 26, 2006, www.psych.ucla.edu/news/russell-poldrack-multi-tasking-adversely-affects-the-brains-learning-systems.
[12] Teresa Amabile, Constance N. Hadley, and Steven J. Kramer, "Creativity Under the Gun," *Harvard Business Review* 80, no. 8 (August 2002): 52.

multi-taskers even performed more poorly on task-switching exercises than their low-media multitasking peers.[13]

With so many demands surrounding us all the time, it's tempting to try to do it all, and all at the same time. The truth, however, is that multitasking actually slows people—and organizations—down. Our brains are optimized to focus on one task at a time. Spreading our attention across multiple tasks becomes draining and leaves little energy for those tasks that matter most. When we switch between tasks, our brains must halt any processing of the current rule sets and load a new set of rules. This happens quickly, but halting, unloading, loading, and restarting take their toll on productivity and our mental and emotional energy. The continuous partial attention we apply to tasks not only results in subpar performance, but it also erodes our energy. It's truly amazing the control that beeps have on our brains—the e-mail ping, the allure of a tweet, and the wonderment of the instant message are consuming the daily supply of brain power. Sometimes, we simply do not have the energy to approach situations in a well-rounded, mindful way.

Perhaps those Genius Grant winners are on to something.

Fear

Another common derailer that is not openly discussed is fear.

Fear is showing up more and more at all levels in organizations, and, in fact, it is *the* most common source of internal noise. Fear of failure, fear of making the wrong decision, and fear of our own inadequacy all affect the actions we take and decisions we make.

---

[13] Randolf E. Schmid, "Study Finds People Who Multitask Often Bad At It," *US News and World Report*, August 24, 2009, www.usnews.com/science/articles/2009/08/24/study-finds-people-who-multitask-often-bad-at-it.

Any initiative can fail. The goal, then, is to fail fast and to fail small, if necessary, and then to learn. This is virtually impossible in most organizations, where deeply rooted biases cloud the system behind the failure, which then distorts judgment and ultimately manifests into fear. Poor decision making creates a vicious cycle—that is, when poor decisions are made, this reinforces an already present anxiety about decision making. As a result, a great deal of time is wasted on undoing or justifying poor decisions, which again creates more anxiety about decision making. This cycle continues and further reinforces an individual's fear to make important decisions. As a result, employees become less likely to step up, share innovative ideas, or solve problems.

If workers are respected for the work they do, why would they go out on a limb to propose and spearhead a new project that may not work? If it fails, they think, all the hard work they did will fall away, and others will see them only as individuals with failed projects.

The fear of failure, rather than the failure itself, becomes the major barrier to organizational growth. Unfortunately, this fear is deep. A litany of factors has contributed to the many limiting beliefs that we all have in the workplace. As a result, our innate abilities are stultified, and organizations are the lesser for it. The truth of the matter is that most executives do want their employees to be innovative, but absorbing the potential consequences from a failed effort can be costly.

Organizations spend a lot of money on training and communications in an effort to reduce fear or to repackage it under the guise of motivation. Regardless, fear remains, and it continues to crop up in new situations and to affect the way individuals and teams collaborate.

The fear of failure incapacitates even the most successful people. There are too many uncontrollable variables in every system to be certain of success. A few years ago, a group of bright young managers were asked by their company's executive team to put together a plan for taking a new product to market. Let's take a quick look at their story.

The company was struggling. The last few quarters had fallen short of projections, and expectations (and pressures) were high for the new product. Instead of being excited about the potential, the team spent most of their first few meetings discussing how they were "destined for failure." They concluded that the executive team did not want to be directly associated with the product, in case the launch failed. This conclusion colored their understanding of their role and robbed them of motivation.

Weeks went by. The team appeared consistently busy, yet made no progress. One team member later commented that during their frequent evening nightcap meetings, they would often bring up documents that reinforced their belief that failure was inevitable. Unconsciously, they were creating a collusive bond to ensure they would not be branded with the failure.

Fortunately, one of the executives noted their frustrations and lack of real progress, and he called the team together. They appeared emotionless as they assembled, as though they were prepared for the worst. He sat down and told them to unpack the crap in their heads. "You were selected because you're the best," he reminded them. "But all the ideas that you've come up with seem safe, lacking both imagination and passion. All of you individually have done great things, and now we need you to think bigger, beyond anything you've tried before. Help us turn this organization around. We need you to focus and challenge one another. I know you can do this and I'm here to help."

By dispelling the negative beliefs that the team was clinging to, the executive was able to turn this situation around. The team members embraced the reminder that they had been chosen because they were the best. It is amazing what happens to the brain when self-depleting thoughts are replaced with positive and purposeful thoughts. The executive's encouragement went a long way in helping the team get refocused and ultimately find a solution.

This story had a happy ending, but that is rarely the case. Often, these situations fester for months and even years, ultimately eroding individual and organizational morale and performance. As my colleagues and I have seen throughout our simulations, no one is impervious to the erosion of morale over time. When the emotional throttle is cranked up and the complexity is high, even the brightest or the most steadfast people become frenzied and make bad decisions and cast blame elsewhere.

With so many derailing factors to distort people's vision, it is often difficult for workers to know which path to take. For managers, leaders, and consultants, the goal is not to control workers' fear, which would be impossible, but rather to help employees be aware of it and learn from it—quickly.

Choice

In an effort to provide consumers freedom of choice, the business community has created an unintended consequence— there are too many choices. This situation inadvertently replaces the liberating feeling of freedom of choice with the burden of selection. A supermarket may carry more than fifty different kinds of cereals, salad dressings, and drinks. Restaurants can configure a meal any way the customer wants. A new car can come loaded with many seductive options. Sure, these are each small decisions, and consumers have now come to expect them. What people are not truly aware of, however, is how much these little choices have a big impact on the important decisions.

The human brain has limited resources and energy to expend to make each choice. In the time between getting up in the morning and going to bed in the evening, an average person makes thousands of decisions. Each choice we make chips away at our mental energy. We have a limited capacity of mental energy and an endless number of daily choices.

"Making decisions takes work," says Barry Schwartz, author of the book *The Paradox of Choice: Why More Is Less*. Schwartz points out, "The mere act of thinking about whether you prefer A or B tires you out." The more choices there are, the more tired and less effective we become. Schwartz continues: "As the number of choices grows further, the negatives escalate until we become overloaded. At this point, choice no longer liberates, but debilitates. It might even be said to tyrannize."

With the onslaught of products hitting the shelves, marketing departments and research institutions across the world are assessing the impacts that too many choices are having on consumers. One such study, which involved 328 participants and was conducted by Kathleen D. Vohs, Ph.D., of the University of Minnesota's marketing department, evaluated the impacts choice has on people while shopping. She found, "There is a significant shift in the mental programming that is made at the time of choosing, whether the person acts on it at that time or sometime in the future. Therefore, simply the act of choosing can cause mental fatigue. Making choices can be difficult and taxing, and there is a personal price to choosing."

Learning how to reserve and apply mental resources is essential for dealing with the increased number of daily choices in a healthy manner.

Noise

Complexity. Obstacles. NOISE. Great ideas—and bad ones—spread like viruses to consumers who are accustomed to making quick judgments. Events around the world unfold within days at the appeal of a tweet. Information spreads so quickly now that we've seen entire countries fall within days, cities within hours, and politicians within minutes. The knowledge acquired by a typical college student threatens to be outdated before she starts her first independent job. We're one generation removed from a college degree guaranteeing employment—but the diploma is no longer a free pass to a career.

Considering the assorted sources of information aggregators that regurgitate messages for the masses, it is no wonder that most people are cautious and untrusting. Knowing who to believe—deciphering fact from fiction—is becoming much more difficult with the volume of information.

On top of that, people are working, connecting, consuming. The piles of reports, endless flow of information, and devices beeping are creating so much noise that, at best, organizations can only merely get people to do their jobs. To squeeze a bit more from people, corporations implement processes and tools at a backbreaking pace. A number of the optimizations do work; however, most just create more noise and further inhibit quality thinking.

Angelika Dimoka, director of the Center for Neural Decision Making at Temple University, conducted a study that measured people's brain activity while they addressed increasingly complex problems (i.e., noise). Using functional magnetic resonance imaging to measure changes in blood flow, she found that as people received more information, their brain activity increased in the dorsolateral prefrontal cortex, a region behind the forehead that is responsible for decision making and control of emotions. But when the load became too much, it was as though a breaker in the brain was triggered, and the prefrontal cortex suddenly shut down. As people reached information overload, Dimoka explained, "They start making stupid mistakes and bad choices because the brain region responsible for smart decision making has essentially left the premises."[14]

This may also explain why people become increasingly frustrated and anxious. Since this region of the brain also controls emotions, an individual's attitude worsens as decision making worsens. This leads to a vicious cycle. The only way to break out of the cycle is to become aware of the impact that noise has on our emotions, energy, and performance.

Noise presents itself in multiple ways. *World noise* is the constant onslaught of news of collapsing governments, wars, uprisings, and acts of terrorism that shape our thinking. *Organizational noise* comes in endless streams of reports, metrics, memos, slide decks, e-mails, tweets, messages, and posts. At the individual level, there is *internal noise*, which manifests from our biases, fears, and too many competing priorities. It's only going to get louder, and leaders need to become increasingly aware of how to help their employees tune in the appropriate information in order to sooth those peaks and valleys caused by the relentless noise.

NEURAL LEADERSHIP

Understanding the reason for predictions

We are wired to predict. That is, when we are in a situation—any situation—we try to make sense of it by predicting what will happen next. For example, when you're watching a movie, reading a report, or listening to a coworker and you encounter a gap, you will most likely predict probable gap fillers. In more complicated situations, you might even run a few "what-if" scenarios in your head to fill likely outcome gaps. The danger in creating predictions is that most are inaccurate or incomplete. With experience, your predictions will improve. However, if you hold

---

[14] Sharon Begley, "I Can't Think," *Newsweek Magazine* (March 2011).

Alfred Shoepenhaver,
on noise

"on the cracking of whips
in the streets at night"

on to a prediction, it may stop you from seeking new perspectives. In other words, you may find yourself jumping to a conclusion and seeking information that confirms your conclusion. It may sound overly simplistic, but knowing you are wired to make predictions might help you suspend your judgment long enough to examine alternative options.

Value Workers

Over the course of one hundred simulated events, my team and I documented patterns of thought that helped us identify individuals we call Value Workers—people who add substantial value in unique situations because they are able to see their derailers and learn new ways to handle them. Because well-designed simulations are both emotionally engaging and intellectually challenging, they drive people to exhibit interesting thinking and behavior patterns.

Value Workers are individuals who have developed the abilities to make better decisions and solve problems collaboratively in dynamic and complex situations. They are equipped to unlearn their biases and relearn quickly as they encounter new and changing situations.

Value Workers:

- Ask good questions to identify the viability of their ideas and the ideas of others.
- Think systemically about change and seek to establish a shared vision.
- Are mindful about their actions and outcomes.
- Draw connections from seemingly disparate sources of information.
- Maintain a big-picture mindset, and avoid jumping from one problem to another.

- Pay attention to patterns and behaviors that help them form a framework for understanding problems.

- Are willing to suspend their judgment long enough to hear other perspectives.

- Don't see failure as something to avoid and tend to make more decisions.

- Surface, collaboratively, their own limiting beliefs and those of the team.

Our goal, beyond identifying thinking patterns, is to develop Value Workers. At The Regis Company, we created the Value Continuum model (Figure 4) to examine the phases that exceptional thinkers and doers go through in their careers.

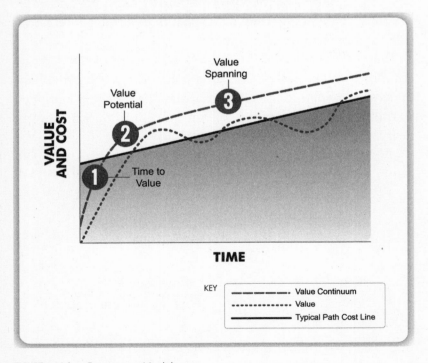

FIGURE 4 Value Continuum Model

The graph depicts the ratio of value produced by an employee to the costs of employing him. When the labeled paths are above the cost line, the value of an employee is greater than the cost of that employee.

First, notice the typical path—a dashed line beginning with a gradual climb that transforms into an oscillating pattern around the cost line. The upward swings are often due to a change in role or a switch to a new company—employees work harder, bring new skills, or are freshly excited about their jobs. The low points are often a result of a market or organization shift and an individual's inability to adapt. In other words, the situation changed and the individual was not equipped to unlearn old habits and learn new ways of thinking.

The Value Continuum path—the solid line—shows an accelerated climb that remains well above the cost line. This path represents an individual whose value is continuously greater than her cost to an organization, that is, the Value Worker.

Most employees do not make it onto the preferred Value Continuum path. While it is natural to face some fluctuation as new scenarios arise and new processes must be created, every dip in an employee's cost/value association affects the company's bottom line. The employees a company needs are not those who require frequent training on minute changes in processes to overcome the latest dip. The Value Workers are those who encounter changing scenarios and adapt.

The numbers on the Value Continuum graph show various points during an employee's career development. Through effective learning solutions, an organization has the opportunity to improve an employee's value in each of these realms.

1. *Time to Value:* This represents the time it takes for an individual to get to a point at which his value is greater than his cost. Today, students coming out of college typically cost more

than the value they provide. The employees who learn to become exceptional thinkers cross the time-to-value threshold more quickly. At this point, an organization can implement new ways of learning that accelerate the development of higher-level thinking and shorten the time until an employee contributes value.

2. *Value Potential:* This represents the value that an individual brings to the organization as new situations emerge over the course of a career. It also shows the potential value an individual can offer an organization at any one point. To prevent employees from oscillating above and below the cost line, an expensive and demoralizing impact, corporations can take steps to develop an individual's ability to think creatively, critically, and systemically. This will result in individuals who can learn, unlearn, and relearn quickly, thus maintaining a steady path on the Value Continuum.

3. *Value Spanning:* This represents the extended value that an employee brings to the organization and to society. Value Workers affect not just their organization, but also the world around them. As an employee's potential increases, her ability to span divisional, organizational, geographical, and cultural boundaries improves and extends out into society. The opportunity here is to broaden employees' perspectives by helping them understand how their individual actions influence the larger system within which they live and work. The result is a Value Worker whose value affects the whole of society.

The path of the Value Continuum model raises two primary questions:

- How does an organization get its employees on the Value Continuum path?
- How does an employee stay on the Value Continuum path?

As my team and I studied Value Workers, we found that these good questions surfaced more questions. Specifically, we became increasingly curious about the skills of these employees and the best methods for developing these skills. We questioned the tug of war between the mere development of important skills and the ability to adeptly apply those skills. We wondered how people can apply the skills of a Value Worker to any situation, whether making a critical decision about the direction of the business or solving a team dynamic issue. Finally, we investigated the idea of feedback. Assuming employees can develop the skills and apply them to any situation, how do they get feedback to further refine the skills?

Our years of working with a range of clients in a variety of simulations have helped us to answer these questions and expand our understanding of the Value Worker. Those employees who stay on the Value Continuum path take part in a virtuous cycle of improving their thinking, applying it to any situation, and learning from the outcome. As individuals go through these phases, they develop their capacity to learn; their mental models are changed, and they experience the Thinking Effect.

What and How

As noted, there are two main thinking paradigms from which people approach the world. The *what-to-think* layer is shaped by events, guided by tasks, and consists of a language that is used to describe parts and causality. The *how-to-think* layer is shaped by patterns and structures and consists of a language that is used to describe systems and relationships.

Developing only the *what-to-think* layer will allow individuals to function effectively only in known and predictable scenarios. In those situations, their performance may be exemplary. But without attending to the deeper level of *how to think*, these individuals will be unable to translate their skills to new, unique, and complex tasks.

The reason many organizational training programs consistently fall short of their promises is because they focus on visible factors, such as outcomes, emotional reactions to a situation, or aggregated data. They address these visible factors by overlaying processes, tools, and procedures that reinforce the *what-to-think* mentality. The irony is that when processes do not produce a change, our tendency is to add more rules and policies and their accompanying metrics, expecting these to be efficient and effective solutions to systemic problems. On the contrary, rules and policies cannot effect drastic change in systemic problems. Instead, they more often lead to the unintended consequence of creating more noise.

I'm not advocating eliminating or even reducing the use of processes and tools. They are critical to the success and safety of many organizations—when used appropriately. What I am advocating is a need to move from simply training people *what to think* to teaching them *how to think*. This shift follows the Value Continuum path, as demonstrated in Figure 5.

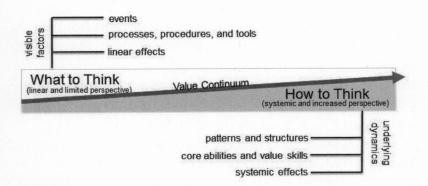

FIGURE 5 What to Think versus How to Think

The primary reason that leaders should help workers move onto the Value Continuum path is that as employees increase their perspective, they increase their value. Markets, organizations, divisions, and teams are all unremittingly connected. As employees move along the Value Continuum, their ability to solve problems, make decisions, and collaborate across geographical and cultural boundaries improves. This happens because their perspective and ability to think differently improve. They move from seeing the world as discrete parts to seeing it as interconnected systems. Instead of seeing a problem independently, they understand it plays a role in a complex system of other problems that all interact with each other. As they move along the Value Continuum, employees begin to offer input that takes all these parts into consideration, increasing the overall value of their output.

In our consulting work, my colleagues and I have seen this happen many times. Individuals come into our simulations with one perspective and leave with multiple new perspectives. Let's take a quick look at an individual who participated in one of our simulations a few years ago.

The simulation incorporated one of our responsive models that encapsulated the primary dynamics surrounding the organization's corporate strategy, external market dynamics, and the typical human factors that contribute to good and bad decisions. The five-day simulation was highly competitive. Within the few first minutes of the simulation, participants sensed that they were part of something different than any traditional training experience. Their adrenaline was high as facilitators explained that were there would be winners and losers. Adding to the excitement, senior executives roamed the hallways listening in to the impassioned debates and reviewed each team's decisions and results every night. There were a few nights that we needed to remind the executives that this was a simulation and they should not react to their emotions.

When this particular individual first arrived to participate in the simulation, he was confident and ready to show us his business skills. Day 1 of the simulation went well for him. Day 2 went even better. However, on Day 3, he drove his team and the simulated business into the ground. He was crushed. His team was crushed. He said he honestly felt that he should be fired, and some of the executives who were reviewing their results shared the same feeling. On Day 4, he and his team spent most of their time together trying to get their heads around what went wrong, because on Day 5 they needed to report out to all their peers.

The simulation experience affected him deeply. It caused him to rethink his approach to leadership and how he ran his division. Recently, he was promoted to a regional position. While we can't take credit for his promotion, we do know that we gave him a significant experience that contributed to his new perspective.

There is a great need for business training to evolve in order to produce a deeper impact. Today, many training departments respond to problems by creating a course that addresses the visible factors. Perhaps an organization needs a visible increase in sales. To procure a fast result, the corporation may train employees to follow a streamlined process proven to result in successful sales. But what happens two years later when this process is out of date in the perpetually evolving business environment? More processes? Better tools? The greater approach is to develop deeper learning solutions that address *how to think*, rather than distilling deep thinking into a few key points.

PATTERNS OF THOUGHT

At The Regis Company, we formed an assessment of training based on our observations and data from more than one hundred different simulation programs delivered globally. We concluded that the majority of training provided today primarily teaches patterns of thought that are consistent with *what-to-think* workers. The participants in these simulations exhibited primarily patterns of thought that are shown in Figure 6 in the What to Think column.

The patterns of thought of Value Workers, shown in the How to Think column, were identified in those participants who performed above average within the simulations. When confronted with complex challenges and bombarded by noise, the *how-to-think* participants collaborated effectively and, for the most part, made quality decisions.

In our research, we began to see that these *how-to-think* patterns of thought, when cultivated, sustainably improve decision making, problem solving, and collaboration. We have since organized and mapped the *how-to-think* patterns to one or more thinking abilities: critical, creative, and systems thinking. We call these the *Core Abilities*, as they are central to the patterns of thought of how-to-think workers and also to all other learned skills.

One way to view the Core Abilities is to think of the muscle groups. Developing core muscles improves overall health, balance, stability, strength, and agility and has been shown to be a primary factor in the ability to participate effectively in most physical activities. In fact, research shows that developing core strength minimizes injuries, results in fewer illnesses, and allows for higher performance in unexpected situations. The comparison transfers over to developing Core Abilities, which are imperative for learning and adapting to new situations. When people improve their core thinking abilities, they improve their effectiveness at making decisions, solving problems, and collaborating, which ultimately defines their value potential. We call these three skills the Value Skills.

What to Think (common patterns)	How to Think (patterns of Value Workers)
• They focus primarily on resolving one issue at a time, without regard to potential systemic effects an action could have.	• They ask good questions to identify the viability of their ideas and the ideas of others.
• They follow processes they have learned, regardless of whether the process fits the scenario at hand.	• They think systemically about change and seek to establish a shared vision.
• They assume that since they observed positive short-term results, they solved the problem.	• They are mindful about their actions and outcomes.
• They quickly jump to conclusions and seek confirming evidence.	• They draw connections between disparate sources of information.
• They appear busy but generate little value.	• They maintain a big-picture mindset and avoid jumping from one problem to another.
• Due to a lack of understanding of the situation, they jump in and tend to make quick gut decisions until things get worse. Then they spiral and become cynical.	• They pay attention to patterns and behaviors that help them form a framework for understanding problems.
	• They are willing to suspend their judgment long enough to hear other perspectives.
	• They don't see failure as something to avoid, and they tend to make more decisions.
	• They surface, collaboratively, their own limiting beliefs and those of the team.

FIGURE 6 Patterns of Thought

Figure 7 illustrates the difference between typical *what-to-think* training solutions and the *how-to-think* solutions we believe are necessary to improve an organization's or an individual's value. The "old way of learning" approach is focused mostly on skill training, less on the Value Skills, and only a small amount on the Core Abilities. With the increased complexity and relentless noise, employees must have the ability to adapt and the capacity to add value. This requires a "new way of learning" in which the focus is predominantly on the Core Abilities and Value Skills.

Soft skills, such as planning, delegating, negotiating, motivating others, resolving conflict, implementing change, driving results, and creating engagement, though typically taught in a workshop or reinforced via e-learning, truly find their roots in the Value Skills and Core Abilities.

I experienced the negative effects of the old way of learning when I first became a manager. I went to a training class and learned a new process and tool for motivating others. I left

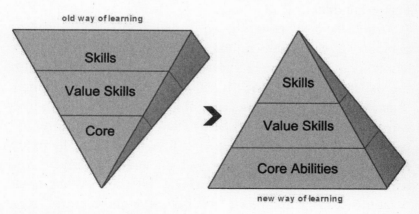

FIGURE 7 Old versus New Way of Learning

excited, and I was determined to be a great coach. I focused on coaching everyone and inspiring them to do great things—until my boss called, disappointed that I'd missed the last few deliverable dates. I then thought, "Coaching is a nice idea, but there's no time for it." So, I took matters into my own hands by doing the work myself. Because I did not understand the underlying relationships between coaching, directing, motivation, and work output, I did not internalize that coaching takes time before it produces any results. So, I implemented a quick fix that resulted in our hitting our next deliverable dates, but I did not build any capacity. As such, I was able to sustain that level of effort for only a few months. I felt deeply frustrated because I had just gone through training but still performed ineffectively. I have seen similar frustration in the new and seasoned managers we have worked with over the years.

The problem is so often the same: leadership programs consistently fail to deliver on their promises because they focus on visible factors and address them by teaching concepts, tips, introspection, and what great leaders do.

But leadership is dynamic. Organizations are dynamic. People are dynamic.

As such, each needs to be understood from a systems perspective within the context of the organization. As Henry Mintzberg, a management and business strategy expert with more than 150 articles and fifteen books to his name, explained, "Sustainable success and successful leadership of an enterprise can be explained by factors other than visible results and the behavior of individual persons." He pointed additionally to the necessity of understanding the systems levels underneath the surface, examining what is "below the waterline." When organizations teach employees how to observe and identify these dynamics at work, they equip employees at all levels to increase their value and better apply other learned skills.

UNDERLYING SYSTEM

About five years ago, my colleagues and I created a process called *impact mapping* to help employees at all levels see and understand the big picture of the organization. Impact mapping is a variation of causal loop diagramming and system modeling. We discovered that unless individuals and teams see the big picture and understand how the various functions or operations interconnect, their actions tend to be both self-serving and short term in their impact.

These issues boil down to a lack of systems, critical thinking, and creative thinking. Failure to consider the entire system and its context often leads to diminishing results over time. Take, for example, understanding leadership dynamics.

The partial impact map shown in Figure 8 provides a simplistic view of the issues I had as a new manager. The map represents human responses (motivation, stress, and performance) to the application of certain leadership skills (coaching, directing, and prioritization).

The circles represent leadership skills, and the boxes represent human responses. The two lightly colored boxes are the results produced (issues, deliverables) by the application of the skills and human responses.

Let's run some mental simulations. Morale is down, issues are up, and the team is falling behind on monthly objectives. As the leader, what do you do? Focus on results? How long can you sustain the team if results become the main focus? Instead, do you focus on doing what is best for your employees? Even well-intended actions can create undesirable results.

Let's say you decide to invest your energy on coaching others. As a result, motivation improves, which causes performance to improve. Consequently, many deliverables are accomplished. As more gets done, your team feels good and motivation further

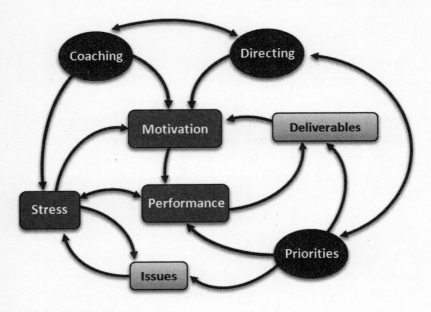

FIGURE 8 Partial Impact Map

improves. At some point, however, the level of performance is difficult to maintain, so issues start to surface. As the issues increase, so does stress, which increases the number of issues and decreases motivation.

When you realize these effects, you begin to split your energy between resolving issues and increasing motivation. This makes sense conceptually, but when your boss calls to express concern that you missed three of your five deliverables, you decide it is time to take matters into your own hands and start directing others more diligently. This crazy cycle repeats, rendering those leadership tools, tips, and tricks impractical.

Each of these choices requires leaders to leverage both the Core Abilities and the Value Skills. The Core Abilities equip you to assess the situation and the Value Skills enable you to take action. The Core Abilities push you to explore and understand the underlying dynamics. Staying at the surface level by reacting to events and trying to fix issues using processes or linear thinking merely creates crazy cycles. These cycles receive momentum from heroic efforts to apply quick fixes. An alternative approach is to recognize the patterns and underlying structures that contribute to the system's behavior. This changes the focus from quick fixes or attributing failure to others to finding ways to improve the system.

This new way of thinking forms a framework for developing *how-to-think* workers.

Actually creating *how-to-think* workers is easier said than done, however. For instance, Core Abilities can't be taught in isolation. They can be introduced or reinforced individually, but to ensure they take root, they must be applied together in an actual or a simulated environment. They are so intimately connected that what is learned at the individual topic level cannot be easily applied when people need to flow between the abilities as a situation evolves. This also applies to the Value Skills. To solve today's complex problems often involves a collaborative effort in decision making.

A NEW TECHNOLOGY FOR A NEW WAY OF THINKING

About ten years ago, my colleagues and I realized that our challenge as training consultants was to develop a technology that would allow us to model the complexities and the noise that reflect the reality of today's organizations. After extensive research, we went down the path of simulations. If designed and executed appropriately, simulations:

- Establish meaning and familiarity to provide a rich, contextually relevant environment in which learning can occur.

- Compress time and space so that cause-and-effect relationships that would otherwise be lost after long delays can be made immediately apparent to the participant.

- Provide an opportunity to observe and record the evolution of decision making, problem solving, and evaluation processes, and to isolate the relevant elements much more easily than can be done retrospectively with real-world events.

- Generate the necessary emotional conditions required to ensure the new learning takes the place of the old learning and replaces inadequate thinking patterns.

- Allow for the presentation of multiple scenarios that expose participants to an assortment of situations to adequately identify gaps in their thinking abilities.

This led to our most important invention, which we call SimGate™. SimGate is used to design, develop, and deliver training in all four quadrants, but its primary capabilities are optimized for developing the *how-to-think* skills and abilities.

Our first simulation created on SimGate was released in 2004 to MBA students. The "Mercury Shoes" simulation consists of five rounds. Each round represents a segment of time, in which a central processing engine, or Responsive Model, presents a set of increasingly difficult challenges. We cover Responsive Modeling in detail in Part II of this book, in the section called Modeling Complexity.

The simulation includes recognizing and responding to the impacts of global competition, multicultural human resource management, domestic and foreign government policy, global marketing, product development, and regional trading blocs such as the European Union or NAFTA. The simulation simultaneously accepts and processes hundreds of inputs and provides robust feedback on the impacts that decisions have throughout the system, including those caused by delayed effects.

We used the simulation to test various hypotheses, all under the belief that as complexity within the system increases, the quality of decision making and the effectiveness of collaboration decreases. We studied team formation and communication, problem solving, responses to ethical decisions, and leadership dynamics.

NEURAL LEADERSHIP

Understanding social needs

All people, regardless of how they like to spend their time, need some level of connection with other people. We are meant to walk this world in fellowship. Over the past twenty years, a growing body of research has begun to describe the brain as a social organ. Many of its functions are designed to process social situations and relationships. In other words, we spend a lot of time thinking about others; frankly, it is very difficult to stay focused on a task without thinking about someone.

Most workplace cultures focus on optimizing results instead of improving social interactions. The unintended consequence of focusing on results instead of people is that, over time, even top performers will feel devalued, will feel less secure, or may even feel unfairly treated.

Using simulations, we've been able to observe various types of team behaviors. Teams who take the time to recognize members and to take a collaborative approach to solving problems seem to inspire others to do the same. The level of energy, enjoyment, and connectedness appears much higher within these teams. Their results are not significantly better than those teams who focus exclusively on fixing problems, but I would assert that over the long term their results will continue to improve, and they will have much higher levels of engagement.

The results of the simulation were truly fascinating. Even when we simplified the simulation by offering only a few decision points, teams learned a great deal about team, business, and leadership dynamics. In one simulation, a participant asked us for permission to fire his entire team. The facilitator wisely counseled him to try to work with the others to resolve issues and problems. At the end of the week, when the team completed the round and "closed the books," the results showed that he had made some seriously bad decisions—completely unaware of his own flawed thinking. As a result, the team asked for permission to fire *him*. Now that's humbling!

The simulations have been most helpful in understanding the limitations that all people have to varying extents when solving complex problems. For example, a common tendency is for participants to fixate on the immediate information within their purview. Even when we provide them with cues into potential future issues or market shifts, they gravitate toward the here and now. Oftentimes, when we ask participants to process their thinking aloud, they firmly believe they're thinking systemically, but their actions within the simulation show otherwise. Typically, when the problem becomes complex, people fixate on only one part of the problem until things spiral out of control. Then they chalk it up as a good lesson learned. However, they still don't understand the need to look at the big picture. Rather, they conclude that they chose to focus on the *wrong* part.

In contrast, great problem solvers seek leverage points that lead to desirable system behavior. They look at the behaviors of the links, or relationships, instead of the outcomes. They don't try to do one big thing; they make small incremental changes while maintaining a big-picture perspective. They realize that the old adage "the harder you push against the system, the harder it pushes back" is very real in organizational systems.

Many of the decision-making simulation programs we use with clients include a dynamically generated impact map (Figure 9), which is a visual representation of the impact that a

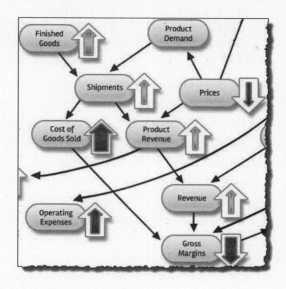

FIGURE 9 Partial Screen Shot of an Impact Map

collective set of decisions have made on the system and how those impacts interconnect. The impact map shows how a team's decisions drove key indicators up or down. The size and direction of the arrows show negative and positive impacts as the result of the decisions made by each team. When participants are shown this map during a simulation, we often observe a behavior we call the "red-arrow syndrome." Typically, early in the simulation, participants become fixated on the largest red arrow. They jump into problem-solving mode and do whatever they can to change it to green, often at the expense of other parts of the system, which shift to red without much notice.

In the sample impact map shown in Figure 9, the big arrow next to "Product Demand" drew the undivided attention of a team bent on increasing market share. The team realized only after several rounds that demand was based on a number of factors, including the size of the potential market, pricing and promotions, reputation, services, and responses from competitors.

They learned that they could not change product demand without understanding how to drive it systemically.

Watching the map change colors from green back to red gave participants their "aha!" moment. Suddenly, the relationships between the parts of the system and the whole system made sense. During the rounds that followed, the team gradually solved more problems and turned more arrows green or reduced the magnitude of the impact shown by the red arrows. This was an exciting breakthrough for our group of trainers, because it gave us confidence that we could actually create real behavioral change.

As I mentioned earlier, it was through simulations that our team began to recognize the impacts of the derailers. We got to a point where we could select, with some certainty, which teams would do well within the simulation based on how well they defined team norms, structured decision making, and treated one another. In addition, we observed that participants who exhibited a sense of awareness of their limitations and those of others tended to collaborate more effectively.

The types of questions participants or teams asked gave us insight into those who would do well in the early rounds, where linear thinking was best, and those who would do well in later rounds, when the complexity increased. For example, teams who approached the challenges systemically asked questions like these:

- "How is this happening?"
- "What would change the patterns we are observing?"
- "How would a new condition influence the systems behavior?"

The most successful teams also established a shared vision and a common purpose. These teams seemed to elicit the patterns of thought that lead to better questioning and collaboration.

REAL CHANGE

As a result of these observations, we started to look at participant behavior over time. The data informed the creation of new design principles and feedback instruments. We now use a design principle called the "emotional throttle" to change team dynamics and participant engagement. By adjusting the throttle, we can influence decision making, collaboration, and a myriad of other human dynamics. For example, simply increasing the amount of information during a round tends to increase team strain and decrease the number of decisions a team makes during that round. Providing too many decision points often prompts participants to resort to guessing, while providing too few tends to cause them to overanalyze or become less engaged.

We also used the data from the early simulations to create new techniques for assessing and providing feedback specific to the Core Abilities and Value Skills. Feedback is essential to help people understand how their actions contribute to the behavior of the systems within which they work. Merely practicing or watching other people's actions is not enough. Individuals don't necessarily learn by doing—they learn by understanding what happened based on their actions (or the actions of others). Usually, the two happen together. People learn something and perform an action, and then they observe what happened (or are informed by it). It is through the process of understanding that insights frequently occur.

Unfortunately, this step into understanding is rarely taken, so insights are formed sporadically at best. This is especially true when dealing with a complex system, since inexperienced people tend to skip the understanding phase or fixate on the wrong things. Feeling confused or overwhelmed, people tend to become indifferent to the results and move on to the next action in hopes that luck will be with them and things may improve. To move people beyond taking chances with luck and into purposeful thinking, we must ensure that they receive multidimensional feedback to help them understand their mental models.

For example, the peaks and valleys shown in Figure 10 depict a system that has varying delays. When we capture participants' decisions and observe them as they think through the effects that contribute to the peaks and valleys, we can identify the behaviors that are creating the oscillation. This deeper understanding leads to insights, which in turn leads to improved mental models.

Coming Full Circle

Before we took any further steps, in the spring of 2004 we decided to put our thinking to the test by circling back to the work of Peter Senge, in his book, *The Fifth Discipline*. As I mentioned in the preface, Peter Senge's book had a profound impact on my thinking. One of his most compelling discussions has to do with mental models. Senge points out, "Mental models are deeply held internal images of how the world works, images that limit us to familiar ways of thinking and acting. Very often, we

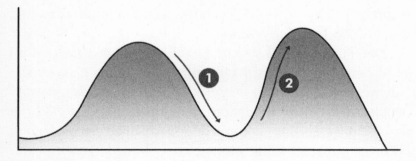

FIGURE 10 Peaks and Valleys

are not consciously aware of our mental models or the effects they have on our behavior." If mental models are not addressed, then it is nearly impossible to develop *how-to-think* workers who are capable of adapting quickly.

Mental models are the lenses through which people see the world and everything in it. They bring meaning to an event, fill in gaps when information is missing, and influence how individuals feel and react to others. Mental models represent how workers see themselves, other people, and the organization. A flawed mental model leads to misunderstandings, incorrect assumptions, and, often, poor decisions.

We all have countless mental models in our heads, making sense of situations, filling in gaps, and applying meaning to experiences. Without our ability to fill in gaps and connect current scenarios to past experiences, our understanding of situations would be significantly depleted. However, because our mental models so often go to work unconsciously, it is very easy for us to react to situations without much thought.

Consider Figure 11, which shows how mental models are constructed. As information comes in from the visible layer, our brain filters and rearranges it, selecting to retain only the

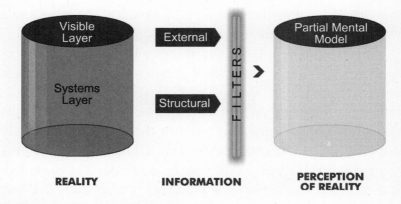

FIGURE 11 How Mental Models Are Constructed

pieces that resonate with our current beliefs. Missing pieces are generated from previous experiences, expectations of what should happen, and assumptions of the current situation. The area below the surface—the systems layer—often does not enter into the construction of our models. We sometimes choose to overlook that level entirely, and sometimes we simply lack the understanding of the system's structure necessary to interpret this portion. The pieces we do absorb from our environment combine with our rationalizations, explanations, and current understanding of the world to form a mental model. As illustrated, the mental model may feel like a complete picture, but in reality, we may have received only half of the picture.

It is only when mental models are challenged that people reevaluate and potentially modify them. In a simulation, my colleagues and I often observe participants who suddenly realize that slightly changing their thinking would produce substantially better results. We have observed that as participants develop their ability to see things differently, they increase their ability to adapt their mental models. This connection makes logical sense, as mental models are built through people's experiences and reinforced as circumstances fulfill their expectations. As shown in Figure 12, we added mental models to the foundation to imply that real learning occurs at the other levels when mental models are changed.

When employees develop the ability to grasp varying perspectives, they simultaneously develop an ability to adapt their mental models to encompass additional viewpoints. In addition, research suggests that as employees increase their systemic thinking abilities, they increase the speed at which they can change their mental models. The rationale is that systems thinking changes how people look at and respond to the world. It makes each of us question why and how things work. In doing so, we indirectly question our own mental models. I've seen this

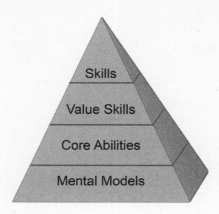

FIGURE 12 The New Learning Solution

happen with my children (yes, I actually spend time every week teaching my children systems thinking) and with coworkers. As Senge points out, "The most powerful learning comes from direct experience."

This phase of our journey has brought us full circle to the core of learning: creating and improving mental models. We have explored the primary abilities that—when developed—create the initial thrust of the Thinking Effect. And now for the next stage of the journey: developing a greater understanding of the Core Abilities, and rethinking how we all think.

PART II

. . . .

Rethinking Thinking

ACCORDING TO A 1997 REPORT FROM IDAHO, thousands of American deaths have been attributed to the chemical compound dihydrogen monoxide (DHMO), mainly through accidental ingestion. The substance can cause severe burns, other unpleasant side effects, and "for those who have developed a dependency on DHMO, complete withdrawal means certain death."

A fourteen-year-old student passed copies of this report to his classmates and asked, "What should we do about this dangerous substance?"

The result was overwhelming: 86 percent of respondents voted to ban DHMO. Of course, the punch line to the study is that none of the students stopped to reason that dihydrogen monoxide—two molecules of hydrogen to one molecule of oxygen—is also known as H_2O, or water, which can indeed result in death from drowning, dehydration, or scalds. The student presented the results of his study as a science fair project under the all-too-apropos title, "How Gullible Are We?"[15]

---

[15] James K. Glassman, "Dihydrogen Monoxide: Unrecognized Killer," *The Orlando Sentinel*, October 28, 1997, http://articles.orlandosentinel.com/1997-10-28/news/9710280246_1_dihydrogen-monoxide-ban-dihydrogen-dhmo.

While we might not all be as gullible as the participants of that well-crafted social experiment, we *are* in fact, *overwhelmed*. Swamped with both information and a whirling dervish of data, most people lack the resources and time to fully consider everything they are told.

When I first read about this experiment, it reminded me of a recent simulation I facilitated in which two participant teams exhibited similar, snap-judgment behavior. As part of the simulation, we invited an "expert" to present during one of the rounds. We told four teams of second-year MBA students that they would compete over several rounds to make their imaginary business the most profitable. Results would be based on the decisions each team made regarding the hypothetical company and global conditions.

Each team received the same setup instructions and data. However, two teams also listened to a ten-minute executive summary from a qualified economist, who had been given the same financial reports and supporting information that the students had received. He distilled that information into a PowerPoint presentation and presented it to those two teams separately.

To our surprise, the economist's summary, while accurate and well-reasoned, did not help the teams at all. In fact, it proved detrimental to their performance. One of the teams that did not hear the economist came in first, closely followed by the other. Both of the teams who heard the economist did poorly in the simulation rounds.

Our observation revealed that the teams who received the executive summary spent no time confirming or challenging the information. They accepted the summary at its surface level and acted with that information as their central focus. Like those high school students who voted before fully understanding the situation, these MBA candidates acted without developing their own understanding of the levers at work.

Some interesting research in Daniel Kahneman's book *Thinking, Fast and Slow* suggests why these individuals so readily accepted information at its surface level. Kahneman, recipient of the Nobel Prize in Economic Sciences for his seminal work in psychology challenging the rational model of judgment and decision making, explains that our brain functions using two distinct systems.[16]

> *System 1 is our fast brain.* We can think of this as our automatic pilot or subconscious brain. It is responsible for getting us through the daily common activities, such as driving to work or brushing our teeth. It is also responsible for quick decisions or judgments. When we receive bits of information, it is System 1 that quickly jumps to a conclusion, filling the gaps along the way.
>
> *System 2 is our slow brain.* It is responsible for analyzing information, assessing data, and considering solutions. As Kahneman explains, we spend most of our time reacting to the world around us through the lens of System 1. System 2 tends to be idling and only kicks into gear when System 1 cannot neatly fit a situation into a pre-established worldview. This reasoning sheds some light on why nicely packaged information is rarely challenged. We unconsciously prefer to slide by without exerting the extra effort required to wake up the Core Abilities of critical, creative, and systems thinking that are triggered in System 2.

---

[16] Daniel Kahneman, *Thinking, Fast and Slow* (New York: Farrar, Straus & Giroux, 2011).

NEURAL LEADERSHIP

Understanding the need for focus

As things become more complex, it takes more attention to deal with them. Yet, we often don't have enough time to pay attention because we have multiple demands that compete for our limited mental resources. This creates a vicious cycle. When tasks compete for the same mental resources, the quality of the results of each task are diminished. For example, while you read this book, you may jump back to your phone to quickly check a new message. When you do this, you pull from similar mental resources. As a result, you don't fully process and internalize either task.

Knowing that your brain is not optimized for multitasking when tasks require the same mental resources, you may want to select one task only and then do it well. Fortunately, you can still ride a bike and sing a song at the same time!

Core Abilities

Despite the value of the Core Abilities—critical, creative, and systems thinking—it is often difficult for people to get a grasp on these essential abilities. Many believe these skills are too difficult to learn and take too much time to apply to real-world problems. Frankly, this is categorically not true. If the right educational methods and reinforcement are applied, every individual can learn to think by using the Core Abilities.

The key point is that these abilities work in concert with each other. While each ability plays a role in the development of initiatives, ideas, and actions, they also serve as a kind of "checks and balances" system. For example, when people apply critical thinking without balancing it with creative and systems thinking, they tend to conduct an in-depth analysis and fit a habitual solution on to the situation. Similarly, creative thinking, if left unchecked, can bring about multiple, potentially impractical solutions to the task at hand—without fully analyzing the outcomes of that solution. Systems thinking balances both critical and creative thinking. By using all three thinking skills, individuals can analyze the situation, create unique solutions, and then assess that information along with the underlying dynamics to reach a point of balanced action.

Ultimately, the three abilities must work in unison to result in an action; otherwise, the thinking becomes merely a task of study. We will explore techniques for developing the Core Abilities shortly. First, let's discuss what each ability means and its unique benefits to help people improve their value.

CRITICAL THINKING

Two of the most prominent researchers and educators in the area of critical thinking are Richard Paul and Linda Elder. In their book *Critical Thinking: Tools for Taking Charge of Your Professional and Personal Life*, they describe a critical thinker as an individual who:

> . . . raises vital questions and problems, gathers and assesses relevant information, and can effectively interpret it; comes to well-reasoned conclusions and solutions, testing them against relevant criteria and standards; thinks open-mindedly within alternative systems of thought, recognizing and assessing, as need be, their assumptions, implications, and practical consequences; and communicates effectively with others in figuring out solutions to complex problems.[17]

---

[17] Richard W. Paul and Linda Elder, *Critical Thinking: Tools for Taking Charge of Your Professional and Personal Life* (Upper Saddle River, NJ: Pearson Education, 2002).

This definition makes intellectual sense, but I must admit that when I first read it I felt intimidated. How in the world will I or other busy people learn to put all of these aspects into practice? The mere idea of performing all of these tasks with every problem or decision is daunting. It would seem that the only way to ensure completion of each aspect of this type of critical thinking is to set it up as a checklist or step-by-step process.

Unfortunately, this is how critical thinking is often taught— as a *what-to-think* process. Employees in a training program memorize a list of steps, test the process against a few case studies, and then return to the job, expected to apply newfound skills across all areas. A few weeks later, these workers are not using the learned critical-thinking processes in their jobs. When a supervisor questions why, a typical response is that there is no clear starting point like the case studies provided. The real world is too complex and is changing far too quickly. It's important to remember that critical thinking is a way of thinking, not a prescribed method or a set of steps.

Let's unpack critical thinking by first looking at what it is not. We need to be careful to avoid confusing critical thinking with fault finding. Fault finding and being critical are used interchangeably. As a result, critical thinking and fault finding are mistakenly associated. People who are fault finding spend most of their energy finding reasons that something will not work. These people often think they are being helpful by breaking down issues and pointing out potential mistakes. Though the intention may be good, the outcome typically keeps others spiraling on the visible factors, trying to correct the surface-level faults pointed out by another.

On the other hand, effective critical thinking does not stop at breaking down; it builds up. The purpose of critical thinking is to understand a situation or problem with the ultimate goal of formulating a solution. Critical thinkers study a situation at the core, analyzing its makeup, cause, and the many factors involved. So, rather than applying a pejorative association, we can equate the word *critical* with *cautious* and *purposeful*.

There's another cautionary tale for defining this ability—don't associate critical thinking with "paralysis by analysis." A common visual image people conjure up when conceptualizing the critical thinker is the wacky professor with his fingers spread deeply into his tangled hair as he labors over piles of data. Ask the pensive professor what he thinks, and he'll reply with qualifying remarks, often leaving people frustrated and without any decision or action plan. In arriving at conclusions (regarding what to believe or what to do), critical thinking sometimes yields equally strong premises on several fronts—and even produces contradictory or conflicting ideas. In these cases, bear in mind that multiple valid conclusions are possible, and it may become necessary to act on one of them before a clear avenue to the best conclusion can be reached.

The act of reaching a conclusion is an important aspect of critical thinking. As I mentioned earlier, for the ability to be effective, it must lead to an output.

What does this output look like? The output of critical thinking is the answers to the questions "Why?" and "How?" This output then feeds into creative thinking to produce a range of options, which generates new questions and further refines the options available until a preferred course of action is reached.

Because my colleagues and I believe in the value of effective critical thinking, we have spent time investigating this Core Ability and developing optimal ways to learn and apply it. We have discovered that at the core of an effective critical thinker is a person who asks good questions. The key word here is *good*. It is natural for all of us to ask questions. Questioning expands our knowledge and exposes errors, equipping us to approach situations with a broader spectrum of information—and therefore be more effective in acquiring and filtering new data. What isn't always so natural (or easy) is to ask *good* questions that uncover the gems just below the surface.

In the business world, individuals and organizations must ask *good* questions, those that can affect the direction a team takes. Not all cultures—including our own—cultivate the innate questioning talents of children, so questions asked by adults tend to settle at the visible layer. For instance, take a car. A visible layer to how a car works is that it has a motor and an engine and you put gas in it, turn on the key, and it works. But really, how it works has to do with all of the interrelated systems that are composed of mechanical parts working together. Understanding a car at the visible layer is just fine; however, understanding why your organization continues to spiral around the same issues year after year requires that you go deeper and understand the interrelated systems.

Information Abuse

This common scenario of an organization that deals with the same issues over and over again is what we refer to as information abuse. Information abuse simply means the dumbing down of information to a point that it is not questioned. Abuse is commonly seen in PowerPoint presentations in which rich data are distilled down to a few key messages. On the whole, key messages that are thoughtfully constructed and articulated can be helpful. These quick summaries are often palatable to our mental models, but they fail to trigger the requisite need for deeper thinking.

Public speakers, politicians, and marketers stake their living on being able to provide information that subtly blends into listeners' understandings of the world without prompting questions or analysis. As long as no internal alarms sound, most of us simply add new information to our bullet lists of knowledge and move on to the next piece of information without asking any relevant questions about its value or legitimacy.

In a working world that is expected to be "on" twenty-four hours a day, many workers have lost the ability to step away from their jobs to think and gain perspective. The result: the accumulation of lots of unprocessed information that clouds judgment and creates fatigue.

Scientists at the University of California, San Francisco, recently released research showing that our inability to process data amidst the constant stream of new information means that much of what we think we are learning is lost. Studying rats, they found that when the animals have a new experience, such as exploring a different area, new patterns of activity appear in their brains. However, the rats seem to process these patterns in a way that will lead to permanent memory only if they take a break from exploring. Scientists reason that the human brain works in the same way. When our minds are constantly stimulated by external sources and bombarded by information, we prevent ourselves from really learning or generating ideas.[18]

My team became intrigued by how these dynamics work together. People in our society are able to echo and repeat more material than ever before, yet we all seem to lack the time or ability to process this information. This phenomenon can be related to Daniel Kahneman's description of our brain's use of Systems 1 and 2. In general, we are relying on System 1 to do our thinking for us. Bombarded with so many choices, it is the only way we can be expected to function on a daily basis. The issue arises when our reliance on System 1 becomes habitual and we don't engage System 2. Or, even if we do kick in System 2, we don't stay there long enough to critically assess the situation.

---

[18] Matt Ritchel, "Your Brain on Computers: Digital Devices Deprive Brain of Needed Downtime," *New York Times*, April 25, 2010. Retrieved September 5, 2012, www.nytimes.com/2010/08/25/technology/25brain.html.

Yet that higher level of thinking is essential to employees and organizations that excel.

A key component to this second level of thinking is that people develop the capacity to filter out information deemed irrelevant or unimportant and focus on the essential information. Otherwise, people become consumed by the information abuse and less effective at guiding and contributing to the organization.

Despite efforts to determine accurate information, however, critical thinkers will always draw upon a framework of principles or experience when interpreting data—a mental model. As previously discussed, unless people are cognizant of these mental models, they can unconsciously enforce biases on the information or task. Mental models can be advantageous insofar as they help individuals structure their analysis and recognize important insights as they examine the data for consistency and gaps. At the same time, mental models can completely distort the truth. The very mental models we trust to help us make sense of a situation may be the same inhibitors that limit us as conditions evolve.

To help organizations become aware of these mental-processing traps and to improve their ability to respond to large amounts of information, our team crafted a series of critical-thinking tools for our simulations. The tools address the perennial problems faced by organizations: synthesis of incomplete and unclear information, and awareness of deeply rooted biases and mental models. With the help of the critical-thinking tools and reflective dialogue, participants practice identifying relevant and diagnostic information from an increasing volume of ambiguous and contradictory data. We throttle the data flow appropriately, and we ask participants to rank and synthesize the information as they're presented with challenges that are reflective of their organization.

For example, the simple text analysis tool shown in Figure 13 assesses a participant's ability to find pertinent information within documents. The tool assesses if the learner selected easy-to-find items or if she was able to draw correlations and appropriately categorize the data in terms of their importance and relevance to the situation. It is important to note that a simulation typically incorporates many of these types of tools to provide participants with varied opportunities to practice and receive more robust feedback. There is a brief overview of key critical-thinking tools in the appendix.

Regardless of the tool our team uses with participants, there are some common behaviors we observe. For example, participants have a tendency to avoid information that might disprove their current working model or might surface questions that may challenge their beliefs. As this happens, we ask them why they selected certain information and overlooked other pieces. Through the process of moving between the various tools and reflective dialogues, participants gain valuable insights into some potentially limiting beliefs.

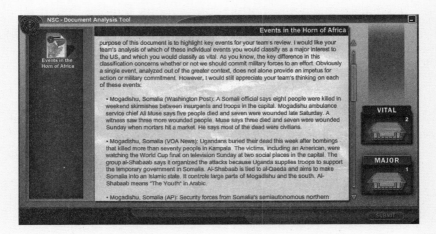

FIGURE 13 Text Analysis Tool

These "aha" moments cross a range of situations from the simple acknowledgment of how participants gravitate toward certain types of information and people, to the realization that they were jumping to conclusions based on limited data, to complete disregard of contradictory evidence because of some ego-centric tendencies.

Another common behavior we observe as participants interact with the various critical-thinking tools in our simulations is that they start guessing when they perceive that situations are too complex. It appears that guessing may be a defense mechanism. For example, when participants are concerned about potentially being perceived as wrong, they toss out a guess. If the guess works, then they feel great. If not, then it was only a guess.

Now, this behavior is not all bad, because guessing within the simulation gives participants a chance to explore the consequences of different options. This often exposes gaps and motivates participants to find something to fill the gaps. We have found that as long as we provide participants with adequate feedback and give them a chance to generate questions, they tend to become more capable as each round progresses.

We have made many other observations, but one that I find the most interesting is how participants give little consideration to market dynamics when generating forecasts. John Sterman, director of the MIT System Dynamics Group and co-faculty at the New England Complex Systems Institute, observed that decision makers often forecast by averaging past values and extrapolating past trends. This makes sense for establishing a baseline, but issues inevitably surface when the decision makers do not incorporate new factors shaping the market into their thinking and forecasting.

Even when we provide the what-to-think participants with market reports, news articles discussing disruptive technologies, or insights from economists, they typically start forecasting by trending historical financials. Now, to be fair, the *how-to-think* participants usually do the same thing, but they also construct a list of questions based on the provided information and use that information to vet their assumptions. Typically, this results in significant changes to their forecast as well as their stated strategy. Because forecasting is such an important skill, we spend ample time moving participants between strategic and tactical decisions so they can see the impacts that each has on their forecasts.

Through practice, participants gradually improve these skills and, as a result, evolve their mental models. Of course, while evolution of a mental model is good, there are times when organizations need revolutionary new mental models. This is where creative thinking is essential.

CREATIVE THINKING

Susan T. Fiske and Shelley E. Taylor, professors of Psychology at Princeton University and UCLA, respectively, found in their studies that individuals often act as "cognitive misers," preferring to do as little thinking as possible.[19] These are the workers who, if given the choice, prefer not to make their own choices or consider their options. It's far easier to go with "tried-and-true" approaches or closely follow a prescribed process. However, this practice does little to add value to a company. Cognitive misers in critical thinking struggle to achieve clarity on their internal business climate and on external business opportunities.

As noted, critical thinking adds value to clearly understanding a situation and effectively analyzing information. Critical thinking equips individuals to understand the parts of a system.

---

[19] Susan T. Fiske and Shelley E. Taylor, *Social Cognition* (New York: McGraw-Hill Higher Education, 2007).

Without critical thinking, individuals resort to habits of viewing a situation, assuming it is exactly as it appears.

However, without the addition of creative thinking, individuals tend to fit used solutions onto new problems. While critical thinking uncovers pertinent data points to weigh dynamic situations, *creative* thinking generates potential solutions. Our research and experience have shown that successful outcomes begin with the proper balance between creativity and critical thinking. Together, they produce a quality of thinking that is fundamental to learning and to the fusion of innovation and execution. These abilities are invaluable to success, for they enable individuals and organizations to escape the trap of becoming cognitive misers.

The tragic truth is that lazy thinking is a learned behavior. We are all born with the desire to learn and think. What parent among us has not been subjected to several hundred "whys" in one day as children carefully observe their environment and question its functioning? Educators observe that most children enter school full of creativity, but this innate aptitude diminishes as the years pass. British researcher Sir Ken Robinson investigated this trend, testing 1,600 children between the ages of three and five on their ability to explore a variety of solutions when generating ideas, a skill critical to innovation. Of these children, 98 percent scored at the highest level. Ten years later, he repeated the test with the same children. This time, only 10 percent scored at the highest level for their age.[20] Somewhere along their educational journey, most children learn to suppress creativity. Far too often, our school systems contribute to this lesson.

---

[20] George Kembel, "The Classroom in 2020," *Forbes*, April 8, 2010, www.forbes.com/2010/04/08/stanford-design-2020-technology-data-companies-10-education.html.

Perhaps the absence of creative thinking from the curriculum of many schools is due in part to the typical mental models people maintain of those who are "creative." Society often presents the stereotype of wacky folks who are brilliant but not overly practical and who may not be desirable employees. It is commonly said that creative thinking is a natural ability—that people are either "born creative" or they are not. Many innovators are in fact uniquely talented people who can see things differently than the rest of us and are able to complete creative feats with no training. But creative thinking in the workplace is a cognitive skill that everyone has to some extent and that everyone can develop. Every individual can learn creative thinking to solve problems and uncover new opportunities.

Organizations who struggle to see the value of creative thinking should be aware that their competition does not. In a 2010 study, The Boston Consulting Group reported that 72 percent of executives, more than any prior year, listed innovation as a top priority.[21]

Without fostering the ability to think creatively, corporations risk being pushed out by the companies that do. As Ray Kroc, the founder of McDonald's, put it, "As soon as you're ripe, you start to rot." Given the pace of our world, unless individuals, products, and ideas evolve and adapt, they become obsolete almost as soon as they appear on the scene.

Of course, the existence of creativity alone isn't enough to generate innovative solutions. Creative thinking must be learned, fostered, promoted, and partnered with a healthy dose of critical thinking. People often look at critical and creative thinking as opposing forces—rational and irrational. A more accurate way of viewing critical and creative thinking

---

[21] "Innovation 2010: A Return to Prominence and the Emergence of a New World Order," The Boston Consulting Group, www.bcg.com/documents/file42620.pdf.

emphasizes that they are meant to exist together—balancing each other (Figure 14).

There is no purpose in creating an idea without critically considering questions of how it will be used, why people will want to use it, and what risks could force the idea off course or obstruct its growth. Critical thinking surfaces the essential elements, while creative thinking considers how to alter those elements. Together, these abilities improve an individual's value and contributions to the organization and ultimately to society.

The problem is that too many people and organizations are holding on to old beliefs.

Popular culture has strictly defined the roles of each half of the brain, labeling the right side the "artistic" side and the left side the "logical." They do have slightly different strengths, but overall our one brain works like an interconnected and inter-dependent system. To argue which hemisphere of the brain is more important is like arguing that the human nervous system is more important than the human respiratory system. It is true that the right brain shows more neural activation during cre-ative tasks, but both hemispheres are involved in thinking. The hemispheres of our brain constantly communicate with each

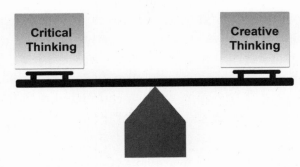

FIGURE 14 Weighing Critical and Creative Thinking

other, and most tasks require the use of both sides. Still, many people hold on to this idea of two brains.

Similarly, we think of critical and creative thinking as independent, discrete skills. The table in Figure 15, adapted from the original work of Robert Fisher in his paper *Creative minds: Building communities of learning in the creative age*, outlines the skills and concepts that we typically assign as opposing factors in critical and creative thinking.

Splitting these skills into two distinct lists promotes the idea that individuals typically fall into one of the two categories— either a critical thinker or a creative thinker. The reality is that we each have the capability to perform both types of thinking. Granted, we may have a propensity toward one, but these traits should not be dividing factors. We are looking at critical thinking and creative thinking all wrong.

There is a deeper reason why critical and creative thinking should be developed together, and that reason is called the *basal ganglia*. The basal ganglia make up a part of the brain that is believed to be active in learning and habit formation. It just so

Critical Thinking	Creative Thinking
Analytic	Generative
Convergent	Divergent
Probability	Possibility
Judgment	Open
Focused	Scattered
Objective	Subjective
The answer	An answer
Left brain	Right brain
Linear	Associative
Yes, but	Yes, and

FIGURE 15 Division of Thinking
(Reprinted with permission)

happens the basal ganglia are located deep within the cerebral cortex between the left and right hemispheres.

Many creative-thinking activities are emotionally engaging, which is important for activating working memory. But working memory holds information for only a short amount of time (while you are actively working with that information). Then those insightful lessons are lost to the onslaught of noise. However, when the critical-thinking parts of the brain are activated along with the creative parts of the brain, associations are formed. Through continued practice, those lessons become part of the various areas of the basal ganglia, equipping thinkers with the ability to flow between analytical and generative, convergent and divergent, objective and subjective thinking.

In the various leadership simulations we've developed, it is clear that good decision makers and problem solvers "flow" between these skills. To help participants practice moving between critical and creative thinking, we created a series of tools and activities. Most of these tools first ask participants to identify the problem, which is often half of the issue in terms of making wise decisions. Learners begin to recognize the need to be thoughtful in how they define a problem. If they're too specific or too broad, they may limit the generation of viable options.

This is why a balance of critical and creative thinking is important. We've found that when assessing a problem, a good decision maker moves between analyzing the parts and generating ideas about the relationships of those parts. In doing so, he uncovers helpful information that exposes the system. Critical thinking provides a means to identify that a problem exists, while creative thinking helps with problem definition. So, as the decision maker looks at the situation from different viewpoints and with varying goals (i.e., analyzing the information at hand, generating ideas about potential changes to make), he begins to see how the various parts interact with each other.

Dr. Robert Harris, retired professor at Vanguard University of Southern California, defines nine perspectives and processes that help to build creativity[22]:

1. *Curiosity.* Creative thinking, like critical thinking, encourages thinkers to ask questions to broaden an issue and expand the boundaries of what they know, rather than digging down deeper into it. Broad knowledge is necessary for creativity to flourish to its fullest. Knowledge is enjoyable and often useful in strange and unexpected ways. Seeking new information does not require a reason. The question "Why do you want to know that?" seems strange to the creative thinker, who is likely to respond, "Because I don't know the answer." The curious person's questioning attitude toward life is positive, not reflecting skepticism or negativism.

2. *Challenge.* Creative thinking challenges the assumptions behind ideas, proposals, problems, beliefs, and statements. Many assumptions, of course, turn out to be necessary and valid, but others are unnecessary or outdated. Creative thinkers root these out and search for alternatives.

3. *Constructive discontent.* Discontent is not all bad. Creative thinking encourages positive, problem-solving discontent that addresses a need for improvement and proposes a solution. Constructive discontent is the first step to identifying problems around us and offering solutions for improvement.

4. *A belief that most problems can be solved.* First by faith and later by experience, the creative thinker believes that something can always be done to eliminate, or at least alleviate, almost every problem. Creative thinkers understand that problems are solved by a commitment of time and energy and, where this

---

[22] Robert Harris, "Introduction to Creative Thinking," July 1, 1998, www.virtualsalt.com/crebook1.htm.

commitment is present, few things are impossible. Creative thinkers look directly into the face of fear.

5. *The ability to suspend judgment and criticism.* To consider all options, creative thinkers suspend judgment about new ideas, have an optimistic attitude toward ideas in general, and avoid condemning them with negative responses like, "That will never work; that's no good; what an idiotic idea; that's impossible."

6. *Seeing the good in the bad.* Creative thinkers ask, "What is good about this?" They can perceive that every idea may have something useful, however minimal that might be, directed to good effect or even made greater.

7. *Believing problems lead to improvements.* Whether we look for issues or not, we know that they will come up. Creative thinking accepts that problems are not necessarily bad if they permit solutions that leave the world better than before.

8. *Seeing solutions instead of problems.* One person's problem can become another person's solution. Creative thinkers can even find good ideas in someone else's bad solutions.

9. *Understanding problems as acceptable risks.* Creative thinkers refuse to hide from problems. They view issues as interesting challenges worth tackling. Creative thinkers may even find problem solving fun, educational, rewarding, ego building, and helpful to society.

Figure 16 demonstrates how participants in one of our simulations apply these different types of creative thinking to multidimensional problems. On the left side of the figure are various work streams that are necessary to accomplish the objectives listed directly across on the right side of the figure. We give participants a library of decision points and actions, as shown at the bottom of the figure. Users must sequence the decision points

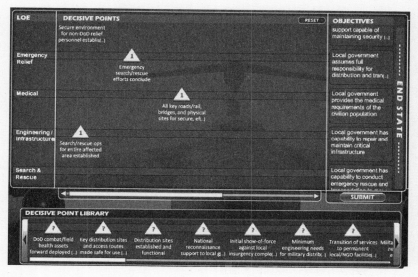

FIGURE 16 Creative and Critical Thinking Tool

by dragging and dropping them on one of the work streams. If participants choose to go deeper, each decision point has additional information. Here's the catch: there are no right answers. Rather, there are many possible solutions, and some decisions at certain times are better than others. Adding to the complexity, the scenario dynamically changes as the situation unfolds. As with many critical and creative thinking tools, the goal is to prepare users to adapt their thinking as new information presents itself by quickly formulating and reformulating recommendations. Through the application of critical thinking, the recommendations are analyzed and judged by simulation engine for effectiveness and appropriateness in solving the problem.

A key component of many of these tools is a reflection on innate biases and fallacious reasoning. Typically, this is accomplished through dialogue with peers or trained facilitators. We've also had success using online collaboration services. The behavior we seek to establish is called *reflective skepticism*, a concept first coined by Dr. Stephen Brookfield. He defines reflective skepticism as ". . . being wary of uncritically accepting an innovation, change, or new perspective simply because it is new," but, rather, having ". . . a readiness to test the validity of claims made by others for any presumed givens, final solutions, and ultimate truths against one's own experience of the world."[23] Reflective skepticism requires checking to see that both critical and creative thinking have taken place—were assumptions identified? Were they valid? Were reasonable alternatives created? Participants in our simulations learn to ask questions such as these:

- What's the problem?
- What are my assumptions?
- What's possible?
- What else?

These questions appear simple, but how often do decision makers even ask them, much less keep at it until they get answers?

When each of us makes these "connections" and flows between critical and creative thinking, we expose flaws in our mental models. Evolutionary changes to our mental models occur when we make connections. Revolutionary changes occur when we create something entirely new, as the situation requires it. Extraordinary changes occur when what we create considers the systemic effects over the long term. This is when systems thinking is most helpful.

---

[23] Stephen Brookfield, *Training Educators of Adults: The Theory and Practice of Graduate Adult Education* (New York: Routledge, 1988), 325.

SYSTEMS THINKING

> The problems of most companies were not brought on
> by competitors or market trends, but were the direct
> result of their own policies. People discover that their
> own policies inevitably generate their troubles. That's a
> very treacherous situation because if you believe these
> policies solve the problem, and you do not see that they
> are causing the problem, you keep repeating more of the
> very policies that create the problem in the first place.
> This can produce a downward spiral toward failure.
>
> —Jay Forrester, in *The Prophet of Unintended Consequences*

A system is a collection of interacting, interrelated, or interdependent parts that form a complex and unified whole that has a specific purpose. Each part of a system plays a role, and the malfunction of one piece can interrupt the flow of the entire system. The concept of systems thinking is a way of seeing the world as a confluence of systems—all systems that influence our daily lives, our organizations, and, ultimately, our actions.

Systems surround us. We are immersed in them. Examples of systems can be found everywhere—ecosystems, economic systems, geopolitical systems, societal systems, and family systems. In fact, we are ourselves a complex system of systems. The world today is intimately and intricately connected, but reductionism is rampant. We are so busy that we reduce complicated scenarios to memorable bullet points and easily definable silos. Given the intricately interwoven nature of our world, this isolated approach to thought is more fruitless and more detrimental than ever.

Compounding the issue is the fact that our brain seems optimized for performing tasks that follow a linear progression.

That tendency is probably why reductionist thinking is so prevalent. We are programmed to think this way, so the concept of systems thinking seems difficult. The remarkable truth is that systems thinking is an innate ability; many of us have simply not exercised it.

I firmly believe that if we were to teach children to think systemically, their brains would be optimized to think systemically about the world. Not only have I seen it with my own children, but I also witnessed it when I observed six Arizona elementary schools that are part of an initiative led by the Waters Foundation to incorporate systems thinking into all academic subjects.

In one of the schools, eleven students met with a trained system thinking facilitator for six months to learn habits of system thinkers. These young adults had been deemed by their school to be problem makers and were all likely to be held back due to their dismal grades.

I was blown away when I watched these young people discuss complicated issues and collaboratively come up with solutions. As they discussed school community issues, they recognized how their own actions inadvertently contributed to the problems. They also took on long-term issues, such as environmental planning, in which they could articulate potential impacts five, ten, and twenty years out. I told my colleagues that these kids would be the envy of many executive teams. Not only did all their grades substantially improve, but also they were no longer destined to be held back, and many of them joined school programs in leadership roles.

Systems thinking can improve overall thinking whenever people are willing to let go of a reductionist past. For employees to really do their jobs, they must understand how their individual actions and decisions contribute to the larger system. This "big picture" perspective helps employees and organizations attain success. In fact, systems thinking is so crucial to Value Workers, it is one of the Core Abilities.

For individuals and organizations alike, systems thinking provides a way to view situations or problems within the context of the larger systems that created them. This viewpoint offers a framework for critical and creative thinking to produce true insights. If creative thinking and critical thinking are like two sides of a scale, then systems thinking is the fulcrum, balancing both creative and critical approaches based upon the situation at hand (see Figure 17).

Systems thinkers look at cause and effect, relationships, feedback, delays, and unintended consequences to find a balance point. Without the balancing effect, creative thinking can become unbound, and an organization may be distracted by chasing too many ideas. Conversely, organizations too heavily focused on critical thinking can get stuck in the perceived need to analyze too much information, creating the well-known "paralysis by analysis" syndrome.

A typical response in either of these circumstances is to focus on better processes and tools for soliciting new ideas and vetting them. These solutions address the visible factors, but the

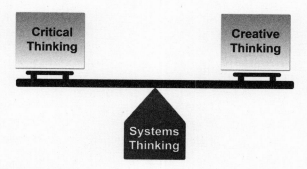

FIGURE 17 The Fulcrum

underlying problem is actually the thinking and attitudes of the workers. Change the thinking and you change the organization.

Systems thinking balances critical thinking and creative thinking by providing context and perspective. In the table shown in Figure 18, I've added a middle column between critical and creative thinking that provides guidance for using systems thinking to balance critical and creative thinking. Thinkers may gravitate to the left or to the right, but the goal is to return to the middle to keep thinking in balance. This balance should also allow thinkers to respond more quickly to certain situations.

Though systems thinking is a natural approach, it initially can be a difficult concept for many people to grasp—and for good reason. A lifetime of learning *what to think* makes any other way of thinking feel uncomfortable and challenging.

Take project management as an example. In my experience, the traditional profession of project management often adheres to nineteenth-century industrial production thinking. High-level project management consists of planning, budgeting, resourcing, scheduling, managing, verifying, and closing, all wrapped

Critical Thinking	Systems Thinking	Creative Thinking
Analytic	Systemic	Generative
Convergent	Concurrent	Divergent
Probability	Feasibility	Possibility
Judgment	Perspective	Open
Focused	Integrated	Scattered
Objective	Underlying dynamics	Subjective
The answer	Leverage point	An answer
Left brain	Whole brain	Right brain
Linear	Structure	Associative
Yes, but	How and why	Yes, and

FIGURE 18 The Connection Between the Two

in documentation, rules, and checklists. In a linear diagram, the process may look like the one shown in Figure 19.

While the goal of this process is to improve performance, the real effect of many complex project management approaches is an erosion of performance. Individual tasks have become so finely sliced as to become almost meaningless. Today's project managers have become laborers in a cubicle, not maestros in front of an orchestra of dynamically harmonizing parts.

Project management from a systems-thinking perspective looks more like the illustration shown in Figure 20, which the interconnected set of activities whose relationships, shown as links, define the outcome between a good and bad project. The common belief is that if a manager performs each activity well, then the project will run smoothly. This may be the case initially, but when problems hit—and they always do—the project manager who has taken the time to think through the links is better prepared to make appropriate and timely adjustments to get the project back on track.

This is the balance between critical and creative thinking. As noted, critical thinking is required to understand all the data generated from the outputs of each of the activities. Creative thinking explores options for changing the inputs or starting conditions of each activity. Systems thinking maintains the big picture: how all the activities interconnect and influence one another over time.

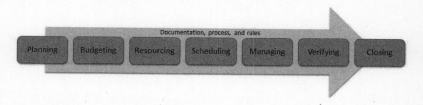

Documentation, process, and rules

Planning · Budgeting · Resourcing · Scheduling · Managing · Verifying · Closing

FIGURE 19 Linear Project Management

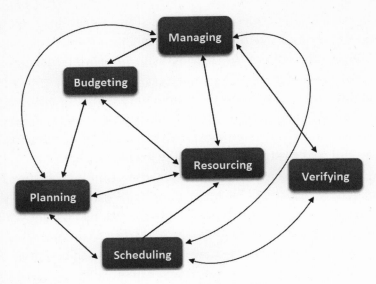

FIGURE 20 Project Management from a Systems Perspective

Being proficient at project management or any other discipline requires a deep understanding of systems thinking. As the next section will show, systems thinking is particularly effective at illuminating two extremely common challenges: feedback loops and delay effects.

Delays and Feedback Loops

Delays occur after it seems the initial results are in. An organization conducts an initiative, assesses the results, and finds that the program is achieving the goals projected. Days, weeks, or months later, a delayed effect can set in, causing astonishing and unexpected results. The longer the delays, the harder it is for people to make good decisions. In our simulations, we noticed a tendency to react to information and make quick judgments. This is true in businesses, but also in everyone's day-to-day lives. Let's take a quick look at an everyday example—a couple's credit card debt—and then see how the same kind of thinking can get businesses into trouble.

Regardless of the reason the couple went into debt, once a debt hit occurs, it can take a long time for them to pay it back due to a delay effect, particularly if most of their monthly income is already going toward "essential" living expenses. The issue exists between the flows (monthly expenses and new debt) versus the debt and ability to pay. First, they have to get the flows in balance again, and then they have to generate enough surplus each month to start working down the debt. So, if they are living 15 percent beyond their means each month, they have to cut their lifestyle by 15 percent just to get the flows to balance, and then they have to cut it more to start working down the debt. So instead of cutting their lifestyle by 15 percent, they might have to cut it by 30 percent for a long time.

Now, take this simple example and think through how delays impact process, decisions, or change initiatives within your organization. Let's say that something goes wrong for your company and the organization mandates a policy. Months or years go by, and now that policy is bad, so a new policy is implemented. Each policy results in changes, but the original reason for the policy is forgotten.

Delays can cause a solution to appear to be working in the short term, only to create very adverse effects at some later point. They can also cause a solution to appear not to be working at all, causing people to give up and retract an action, or to put unwarranted effort into that solution.

Delayed effects lead to oscillations, which are visible in business, economics, and power, among other areas. An effective way to understand them is through the use of simulations, which can be even more successful as a teacher than real-world experience can be, since it is often difficult for learners to connect actions to outcomes that occur only months or years later.

That gap is one big reason why it is so difficult to hold people accountable for their actions in the workplace.

Adding to the complexity are *feedback loops*. As noted, a traditional way of viewing the world involves linear cause-and-effect understanding: event A causes B causes C, and so on. A systems view of the world takes this a step further by showing the interrelationships: it identifies where A affects B and B in turn affects A. In this view, the connection back to A from B is called *feedback*. As A shapes B, B gives A feedback that will further shape A. This reinforcing loop grows over time, producing something that is either desirable or undesirable.

Feedback loops exist everywhere in life and throughout organizations. Unfortunately, they can be difficult to understand without a systems perspective. Organizations may overlook them unless they take the entire system into consideration because a small alteration can appear nonthreatening. However, when a change continues to expand due to a feedback loop, it will ultimately affect the company.

There are two types of feedback loops: positive (or self-reinforcing), which create effects throughout the system that cause the part to get larger; and negative, which create effects throughout the system that cause the part to get larger. For example, a positive loop happens when consumers become aware of your product. Your organization produces more product, which then increases the number of consumers who gain access to it. A negative loop kicks in when your consumer base grows too quickly, causing a heavy demand for your product. This then strains your organization's capacity to produce quality products in a timely manner, which then frustrates your consumers, and your market begins to shrink.

Feedback loops can provide engines for growth, as success breeds success and satisfied customers attract even more new customers. Or they can create limits to growth, as it becomes progressively harder to tap the remaining market or get one more product out each year. Either way, feedback loops are capable of creating significant unintended consequences.

So, learning to think systemically can be an involved undertaking. You may be wondering if it is worth the investment—just how often will you or your employees use systems thinking?

Michael Goodman of Innovation Associates Organizational Learning, in partnership with isee systems, a leading provider of systems modeling software, put together an online course that offers a helpful summary of when to use systems thinking and when not to use it (Figure 21).

This tongue-in-cheek chart makes a powerful point. Systems thinking is a valuable thinking skill across all areas of a business. For an organization to adapt, it must equip employees to understand the full system of which they are a part. Only when they grasp the interconnectivities in an organization and in the world

Do use systems thinking to:	Don't use systems thinking to:
• Identify or clarify a problem.	• Impress people or win an argument.
• Increase creative discussion.	
• Promote inquiry and challenge preconceived ideas.	• Validate prior views.
• Bring out the validity of multiple perspectives.	• Hide uncertainties.
• Make assumptions explicit.	• Blame individuals.
• Sift out major issues and factors.	
• Find the systemic causes of stubborn problems.	
• Test the viability of previously proposed solutions.	

FIGURE 21 When to Use Systems Thinking
(Reprinted with permission)

will they truly understand how to function within those systems. Systems thinking creates a culture where individuals naturally consider their actions and decisions on a much larger scale.

There are many other dynamics at work, but understanding the illusiveness of delays and the impacts of feedback loops are enough to appreciate the importance for new approaches to thinking. System dynamics take interdependencies and moving parts into account, promoting a greater understanding of how actions within one part will affect the entire system.

Modeling Complexity

Sounds straightforward, right? Develop the Core Abilities and, in doing so, you improve your ability to develop new mental models and add value. But this is only one aspect of creating the Thinking Effect, and it happens to be difficult to put into motion using traditional approaches. Most of the methodologies, technologies, and resources available to organizations are best suited for teaching people *what to think*. Even leading simulation technologies are far too limited in their ability fully to model the dynamics and complexities of organizations. Take, for instance, two of the most common simulation engines: decision trees and spreadsheets.

Decision Tree Engine: Decision trees are simple branching logic trees. If the participant chooses one action, he will be sent down a predetermined path. If he chooses another, he will be sent down a different predetermined path. Decision tree engines are limited in that they cannot determine how events occur in relation to other events. For example, a decision made in one division of a company within a decision tree engine will have no bearing on the other divisions of the company (even though, in reality, different divisions affect one another all the time).

Rethinking Thinking **93**

Because of the predetermined nature of these engines, they typically are best suited for simulations that focus on working step by step through a problem.

Decision tree simulations do not provide individualized feedback or alter the scenarios based on a participant's actions. With this type of simulation, several participants could have basically the same experience, as there are only predetermined options and outcomes. So, if you want your employees to always think and respond in narrowly prescribed ways, this can be a useful tool. A decision tree engine has limited facility to teach the Core Abilities, but it can accomplish the goals of training for some jobs in some companies, such as improving customer relationship skills or learning a new methodology.

Spreadsheet Engine: Spreadsheet-driven simulations are the most common technologies used to create financially driven simulations. Spreadsheets perform well when they are used to model linear systems, but they are poor at modeling complex systems. Simulation developers find them costly to build, so most spreadsheet-driven simulations are built for one purpose and tailored for other uses, which requires a seasoned facilitator to help participants make connections and provide feedback. For example, a solution may be created to teach financial acumen, and then lightly tailored and reapplied to teach strategic alignment. These black boxes fail to help participants see the big picture and explore the interconnected system behind their decisions and actions on the job. So, if the primary goal is financial acumen, then spreadsheet engines provide a good foundation. However, their ability to teach the human dynamics in the context of business dynamics is limited; thus, they are not an optimal option for developing the Core Abilities.

Human dynamics, feedback loops, delays, and interdependencies are fundamental to how people think and respond to an organization. And, being able to implement these engines quickly and cost effectively is paramount to an organization's budget. As such, my colleagues and I recognized the need for a new technology that would allow us to model organizational and human dynamics quickly and cost effectively. Working with individuals from MIT and leading system dynamics modelers, we created a new technology we call Responsive Modeling.

Responsive Modeling combines system dynamics and agent-based modeling to create an adaptive environment to challenge students to think differently. We call it Responsive Modeling because the models respond to student, organizational, and market inputs and outputs. Responsive Models have been built for processes as simple as staffing a small restaurant and as complex as the interconnections between dozens of divisions of a multinational organization.

Responsive Modeling has also been used extensively with executive teams to develop shared mental models of how an organization works within its broader system, and to test various "what-if" scenarios. This technique has helped shape organizations of all sizes and types. Responsive Modeling provided my colleagues and I with the solutions we had been looking for to create an environment that closely approximates reality. It now gives us a tool to use with executives to create a shared vision, and it serves as an engine behind our simulations to challenge the broader audience to test their ideas and perspectives.

RESPONSIVE MODELING AS A TOOL

The modeling process is one of the most insightful business tools an organization of any type can use to help evolve employees' thinking.

Rod Walker, one of the top systems modelers in the world—a claim he would never make himself—explains that when work teams are exposed to models, they have the opportunity to better understand causal factors, dynamics, and perhaps the reason a problem has never been solved. Modeling allows teams to explore the dynamics of a system and various strategies for handling them. It also helps build consensus. When faced with a major decision, Walker says, many of the people within an organizational system understand at least some of the problems. For example, a vice president of sales may understand issues pertinent to new product sales but lacks the insights into operations. As a result, it is difficult for everyone involved to learn what they should from each other and reach consensus on complex systems without a visible framework.

In an organizational context, a systems model helps employees understand their company as a whole as well as the parts, and helps them take personal accountability for the quality of their work and the impact of their actions and decisions. For example, in a systems model, a manager could foresee that cutting staff will slow productivity per person or labor hour, as remaining employees carry extra loads and worry about their own job security.

The model creates a more organic picture of the business that accommodates unexpected situations or combined decisions. Many companies use charts, graphs, process diagrams, and procedure documents to explain individual aspects of their business. These traditional tools can be helpful, but they aren't enough. In the real world, sales, marketing, production, and distribution are all interrelated and interdependent. Four separately developed charts, no matter how cleverly designed, will fail to show these relationships, which is paramount for developing the Core Abilities.

Models can help students analyze and understand a specific initiative or process or see how an entire enterprise functions as a system. As a manager, leader, or consultant, you can use models to help workers explore future states, needed resources, and possible pitfalls. Roles, functions, and performance tasks can be tested against the strategy of the organization. Models help learners to evolve ideas in a safe but realistic environment. This is essential for developing critical-thinking skills.

Rethinking Leadership

If you take a deeper look at organizational structures and organizational process, you will see that their design supports discrete thinking. That is, employees focus on isolated divisions, programs, or issues, rather than the big picture. There may be some overlap of objectives between divisions that roll up into an organizational scorecard, but the fact is that people will do what people do best—jump in, solve the problem at hand, and drive up their results. Hence, the silo effect that many organizations experience.

A few years ago, my colleagues and I worked with an organization responsible for medical practices across the United States. By using responsive models, they were able to gain a tremendous amount of insight that led to significant changes in its processes, policies, and leadership. Since medical practice managers have to make a complex set of decisions with competing interests related to quality of care, capacity, staffing, collections, and cost management, the management team in this case needed to get their heads around making tactical decisions while keeping an operational and strategic focus.

The responsive model that the team used is shown in Figure 22. It provided results of the competing decisions and rich feedback reflecting difficult trade-offs. The management team received feedback on how morale might change over time relative to their decisions. We provided them with detailed information about staffing, possible effects of turnover, and operational efficiencies, such as improving processes or implementing new technologies. In addition, the model generated insights into

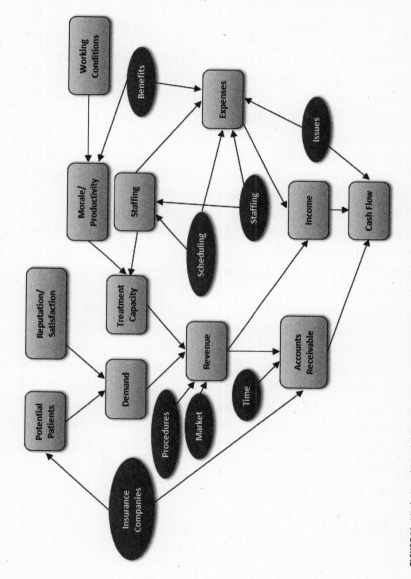

FIGURE 22 High-Level Model Drafted During the Initial Design Phase

possible limits to growth and potential impacts to key performance indicators.

During the development of the model, it became apparent that each of the executives had a different perspective on
how a medical practice must operate. Working closely with the
executive team, I guided them through an interview process
that helped them craft their own plan in relation to the organization's stated strategy. It was enlightening to see how each
person interpreted the organization's stated strategy differently.

Responsive Modeling helped evolve the team's thinking and
perspective by showing the interdependencies of the various
divisions of the organization. Each executive at the medical
practice was able to test out personal assumptions, try different scenarios, and evaluate the potential outcomes across the
various divisions. During the process, they agreed on some fundamental policy changes.

The most impressive learning, from my perspective, was how
they individually and collectively reevaluated their approach to
leadership. As one of the executives stated, "It appears that if
we incrementally improve work conditions and update a few
dated processes, we will see an uptick in performance. However,
our greatest leverage point to creating sustainable change is to
rebuild our community mindset that by serving one another, we
can better serve our patients." Responsive Modeling has become
an invaluable tool for scenario planning, supporting decisions,
and understanding complex problems.

Redefining Value

It seems likely that the capacity to tolerate uncertainty
has something to do with how our participants behaved.
When someone simply walks away from difficult
problems or "solves" them by delegating them to others,

when someone is all too ready to let new information distract him from the problem he is working on at the moment, when someone solves the problems she can solve rather than the ones she ought to solve, when someone is reluctant to reflect on his actions, it is hard not to see in such behavior a refusal to recognize one's impotence and helplessness and a tendency to seek refuge in certainty and security.

Dietrich Dörner, *The Logic of Failure*

In a society so fixated on one million-dollar word, *success*—how to be a success, teaching students to be a success, measuring success—the definition has become muddled. Is success defined as money? Fame? Happiness? A promotion? This vague goal hinders action. "Strive not to be a success, but to be of value," Albert Einstein said. Almost a century later, his message rings true. Organizations of the future must shift their focus away from success to the idea of value. The outcome benefits both the organization and the individual.

Historically, a company's value was defined by its income statements. Value increased if it made more money than it spent, if it kept a carefully controlled inventory, and if it appeared to be growing. Busy offices full of conference rooms and stacks of paper looked like successful endeavors. Selling the widget was the first priority, and the most valuable employees were those who followed the script and generated the most profit.

But then the digital economy emerged, the world got noisy, and the concept of "value" changed. Today, organizational value has become a measurement of how we think, not what we do. Value is becoming a determinant for the types and quality of people an organization attracts. It is becoming an indicator of how quickly an individual can unlearn and learn.

The Value Skills are not just something organizations can hope individuals will develop over time through experience. This process is too costly and too slow. Rather, the focus should be on creating business-relevant experiences that allow employees to practices the Core Abilities in a variety of situations across a spectrum of organizational challenges.

The graph shown in Figure 23, adapted from Peter Cappelli's research depicting the ratio of value produced by employees to the costs of employing them,[24] depicts the ratio of value produced by employees to the costs of employing them. There are three phases. Phase 1 represents the time in which someone is just learning a new job. Phase 2 depicts the time in which someone not only knows how to do the job, but also does more than what is expected. Phase 3 represents the period in which the job has significantly changed and the individual has not kept up with the changes. Peter Cappelli, Professor of Management at the Wharton School and author of *Talent on Demand: Managing Talent in an Age of Uncertainty*, observed that over the past few decades, organizations have been finding ways to optimize Phase 2. They minimize Phase 1 by "buying talent" capable of quickly moving into Phase 2 and adding value, rather than investing in training. This is a great strategy for the short term, but as Cappelli points out, companies offering higher salaries to "buy" talent away from the companies that trained them may be contributing to the unsustainable salary surges seen today.

The logic is that the "buyers" could offer more salary because they didn't need to recoup the investment that the other company made during the first phase. But when the cycle is recognized, competitors react by increasing salaries internally to avoid losing talent. In the end, both sets of companies can find

---

[24] Peter Cappelli, *Talent on Demand: Managing Talent in an Age of Uncertainty* (Harvard Business Press, 2008), 116.

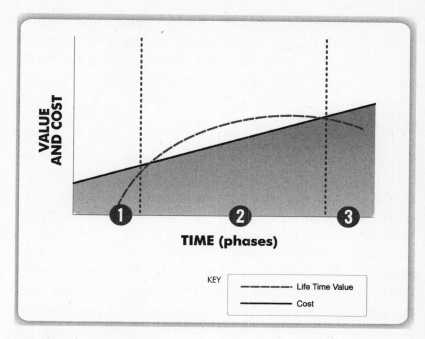

FIGURE 23 Ratio of Value to Cost
(Reprinted with permission)

themselves with very expensive employees who add marginal value.

There are people who are worth their cost, but on the whole, raising the cost line without raising the value line is unsustainable. It adds to the fear, which is part of what causes many organizations to look toward outsourcing, automation, and global partners.

There is another way to proceed: developing the talent within the organization. This is what prompted us to create the concept of the Value Worker—an individual who expands her ability to learn and her capacity to add value beyond the job description.

But how should organizations develop these workers' talents? Instead of trying to "boil the ocean" by creating huge catalogs of courses, following unwieldy competency models, and jumping on the next technology bandwagon, a more prudent approach is to focus on the three skills that generate (or impede) value: decision making, problem solving, and collaboration.

DECISION MAKING

In a 2010 article in *McKinsey Quarterly*, authors Don Lovallo and Oliver Sibony examine a recent survey of 2,207 executives, in which only 28 percent said that the quality of strategic decisions in their companies was generally good. Another 60 percent thought that bad decisions were made about as frequently as good ones, and the remaining 12 percent thought good decisions were made altogether infrequently. With that many bad decisions hindering organizations, the McKinsey team set out to quantify the financial value of quality, unbiased decisions, and to create a common language for how to define good decisions.

They studied 1,048 major decisions made over a five-year period. Isolating factors such as industry, geography, and size, they calculated the variance between decision outcomes, the quality of the decision-making process, and the quality of data analysis.[25] They concluded that people make better decisions in the workplace when they are encouraged to recognize their personal and professional biases, examine broader alternative hypotheses, and appreciate uncertainty.

An examination of the broader community of researchers and research reveals that there are a few common tenets to improving decision making. Decision making is best learned in the real-life contexts of an organization. It's not possible to teach people to become better decision makers by describing

---

[25] Dan Lovallo and Oliver Sibony, "The Case for Behavioral Strategy," *McKinsey Quarterly*, March 2010, www.veruspartners.net/private/app/webroot/files/cabe10.pdf.

decision-making processes, providing checklists, or punishing failures. Employees improve their decision-making skills the most in the context of real-world situations, in which they have time to reflect, evaluate, adjust, and reevaluate the impacts of their actions.

The McKinsey study went on to show that when organizations focused on and improved decision-making skills, their return on investment (ROI) improved by 6.9 percent.[26] Now, that's a new way of thinking about value.

PROBLEM SOLVING

If decision making is the skill that workers need daily, then problem solving is the one that, all by itself, can really increase the value of an organization.

Ask almost any executive leader what kind of employee is needed the most, and you will hear "problem solvers." Chances are, that executive got to where he is today either by being good at solving problems or by being surrounded by people who were good at solving problems. The best executive knows that employees at every level are called on to solve internal, client, or customer problems, or to help others solve problems. Even as day-to-day operations are automated and streamlined, problem solving is a skill that requires a worker.

Problems typically have many attributes, considerations, and solutions, each with its own spectrum of possible outcomes. Problem solving is considered the most complex of all intellectual functions, a higher-order cognitive process that requires the modulation and control of more routine or fundamental skills. In fact, problem solving requires a combination of critical,

---

[26] Lovallo and Sibony, "The Case for Behavioral Strategy" (*McKinsey Quarterly*: March 2010).

systems, and creative thinking, as well as the value skills of decision making and collaboration.

There are problems that have "correct" solutions and problems that do not have any solutions. As in decision making, the mindset of solving problems is more important than the solution, and learning how to think differently in novel situations is key to successful problem solving.

As Peter Senge wrote, "Today's problems come from yesterday's solutions." There are often so many interdependent factors contributing to a problem that "fixing" one aspect of the problem may cause new problems. A valuable employee is one who internalized this thinking about approaching problems.

COLLABORATION

The golden thread that ties all the Core Abilities and Value Skills together for a common purpose is collaboration. Globalization, mergers, and acquisitions in an increasingly competitive market require leaders and workers to learn the art and discipline of collaboration across organizational and cultural boundaries, uniting people from diverse backgrounds.

Regardless of the challenges, one of the most effective ways to solve problems is through the collaboration of diverse thinkers. At the core of collaboration is a collective determination to strive for something greater than any individual can achieve alone. It requires a willingness to share and learn. When collaboration is done right, teams that work collaboratively can leverage resources more responsibly, solve problems more thoughtfully, and find new ways to do things more innovatively.

This all sounds like a no-brainer. Of course collaboration is important. Why, then, with so much written about the subject and so much of our daily time spent practicing communication, can most problems be traced back to a breakdown in communication?

It's because organizations are teaching and practicing the wrong skills or they talk about the purpose of communication in abstract terms. For example, most training talks about the need to establish trust and credibility before real communication can occur. Other programs focus on processes or tools used to drive toward win/win outcomes. And others focus on what is needed to engage the hearts and minds of the listeners to persuade and motivate them to do your bidding.

Frankly, it's hard to argue with any of these statements. On the surface, they're all important to communication. The issue resides in the fact that they focus on the visible factors of communication and miss the underlying dynamics that drive effective collaboration.

Communication, in its simplest definition, implies that the communicator conveys information to the receiver, who then reciprocates with either questions or confirmation. This process switches between the various parties until understanding is achieved.

Collaboration, as we define it, focuses on the identification of one's own biases and flawed mental models that hinder the progress toward a shared vision. While communication emphasizes external processes, collaboration exposes internal dynamics. Both are needed, but the latter is rarely developed. Effective collaboration, then, is not just about getting others to agree; it resides in the ability of the collaborators to surface and discuss the underlying systems behind the problem. If the focus is placed on the system, then less blame will be placed on individuals, allowing for more productive dialogue. This is critical. Because of democratization and new media sources, the number of people involved in making decisions is significantly increasing, which means the likelihood of gaining agreement will continue to become more difficult. Therefore, value workers will be those who can collaborate across boundaries (divisional, geographical, or cultural) to make decisions that lead to systemic solutions to problems.

In their research titled "Discovery Mindset: A Decision-Making Model for Discovery and Collaboration," Joy Benson and Sally Dresdow found that ". . . decision makers need to expand not only their frame of reference but also their mental model of what constitutes effective decision making. Doing so can help them be more effective in leading and in the process of discovery that is focused on expanding the search for ideas and exploring multiple alternatives. It also encourages the collaboration and engagement of those affected by the decision making process and outcomes."[27]

I'm guessing, at this point, that there may be a reader who is saying, "Yes, but what about . . . ?" There are other important skills, but at the end of the day an individual's value is ultimately determined by the problems she solves as the result of the decisions she makes collaboratively.

NEURAL LEADERSHIP

Understanding the need for fairness

After ten years of watching participants battle it out in simulations, I am convinced that people will fight for fairness above glory. Let me clarify. Teams will be very competitive and do what it takes to win. However, teams cannot achieve unanimity until all members feel they have been treated fairly. Now, individuals may give in or agree to disagree so that their team

---

[27] Joy Benson and Sally Dresdow, "Discovery Mindset: A Decision-Making Model for Discovery and Collaboration," *Management Decision*, 41:10 (2003): 997–1005.

might go on to victory, but in doing so, the team as a whole will have lost the larger battle. Unless the underlying need for fairness is established and upheld for everybody, nobody wins.

Neuroscientists have discovered that when people feel as though they have been treated unfairly, there is activity in the amygdala, which performs a primary role in the processing of memory and emotional reactions. Inidivuals will remember being treated unfairly when they interact in a similar situation or with a similar person. People don't have to go far to recall a time or two when they felt as though they were treated with disrespect, were not listened to, were overlooked, or were labeled and put into an invisible box. The feeling of fairness is so important to the brain's well-being that a person may choose fairness over other external rewards. Understanding this innate need is helpful in creating relationships that focus on respect, acceptance, and equality.

Case Study

Several years ago my colleagues and I were asked to work with United Parcel Service (UPS), which was planning to restructure its US Package Operations Department by consolidating forty-six districts into twenty, a change that would significantly affect the company's district leadership.

As we discovered, there were many challenges inherent in the change:

- Getting newly formed teams with diverse biases, backgrounds, and mental models to collaborate on how to grow and run a district.

- Moving from a culture where most decisions were made by the corporate office to an increased span of control at the district level.

- Evolving the managers' approach from general cost management to a true Profit & Loss focus.

- Developing an understanding of the short- and long-term trade-offs regarding market segmentation, pricing, value positioning, and globalization.

Most of the team members who participated in our simulations were UPS veterans, well versed in the old environment. Few participants had much exposure to the new business model. Their success depended on shifting from a tactical to a more strategic approach, collaborating with different team members in new areas, and changing deeply engrained habits.

Company executives recognized that merely telling district teams what to do was insufficient for them to succeed in the challenges ahead. Instead, Stephen Jones, Corporate Training & Development manager, created a vision for a leadership simulation that would span a hypothetical three-year time frame, in which participants could make decisions and follow the impacts of decisions over time. The first step in our process was to create a responsive model that represented both the current and future state of UPS.

The model was loaded into SimGate, along with market data, global conditions, and company reports (see Figure 24). The simulation required teams to analyze data, set strategies, make both strategic and tactical decisions, and see the performance of the district across many indicators. Time was limited, and teams had to rely on each other to recommend approaches.

The most powerful way to get a diverse group of people together is to give them a difficult problem to solve. In this case, individuals who had never worked together and who were responsible for different parts of the business needed to quickly establish team norms and tackle some very difficult problems.

Because this initiative was so important to the business, the simulation spanned seven days. Each day, teams faced different challenges as they experienced the consequences of decisions

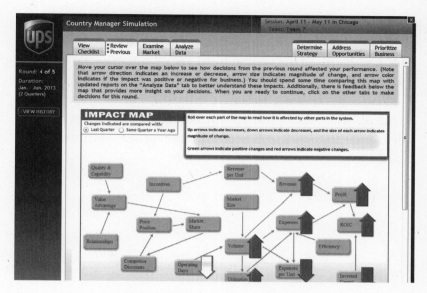

FIGURE 24 Screen Capture from the UPS Country Manager Simulation

made the previous day. The emotional throttle was set very high in this particular simulation. By the third and fourth day of the simulation, participants were no longer giving high fives for coming out ahead of other teams. Instead, they were trying to unpack why their division was spiraling out of control or how they had reached certain limits to growth.

We gave teams ample time to process and reflect on their decisions and team dynamics between the various rounds of the simulation. At the conclusion of the week, teams presented and defended their actions, discussed how they would approach things differently, and outlined steps they would need to take to further develop the team.

Anne Schwartz, Vice President of Global Learning & Development, explained that the simulation was instrumental in accelerating the UPS regional transformation. "The simulation is part of our learning ecosystem. Much like a biological ecosystem in which physical biological organisms interact with every other element, a learning ecosystem integrates both business and learning components to create an adaptive learning environment."

The restructuring initiative continues to be measured in terms of impact on profitability, revenue growth (by market), sales, and customer indicators. Initial results have been very positive.

PART III
·····················

Rethinking Learning

NOT TOO LONG AGO, a unique book hit the shelf. As a ninety-six-year-old, James Henry was illiterate. Over the course of his life, the career fisherman had managed to navigate through a written, word-heavy world by using tricks. When eating out, for example, rather than read the menu, he would echo the order of a companion. Even his close friends didn't realize his secret. Then at ninety-six, nine decades after most children begin reciting the alphabet and spelling their names, Henry learned to read. Two years later, at ninety-eight, he wrote a book about his life titled *In a Fisherman's Language*. The book has become internationally recognized, a testament to the often-dismissed truth that we are fully capable of learning throughout our entire lives. Though we make a habit of claiming to be "too old" to learn new concepts or to try new activities, our brains remain active, perpetually ready to develop further.

This realization is great news for organizations that hope to develop Value Workers. It means that employees—even people in the middle or late stages in their careers—can change, grow, and adapt. And it means that we often sell adults short. Even as we age, our brains are capable of doing far more than memorizing processes or concepts. For most of the last century, the pre-vailing belief among neuroscientists was that our adult brains remain relatively static. For instance, Nobel laureate Santiago Ramon y Cajal postulated that in the adult brain neural path-ways are "fixed, ended and immutable."[28] Children, researchers thought, were equipped to learn and form new habits, but adults were not.

Recent studies have turned those ideas upside down. Chil-dren do not have more memory-based neurons than adults, as scientists originally assumed. In fact, a 2011 report from The Dana Foundation states that the hippocampus—the structure that's so important to memory—maintains a steady supply of its principal cells across a person's lifespan.[29]

The brain's ability to adapt its structural and functional organization as a result of experience is called *neuroplasticity*. Adaptations range from cellular changes due to learning, to large-scale remapping as a result of injury. Understanding neu-roplasticity is essential for developing training that is meant to change behavior.

The question now: How do we shape the desired changes in our brains? Most workplace training fails to achieve its objec-tives because it is limited in its ability to alter the brain structure necessary for changing behavior. When people receive informa-tion passively—such as when someone tells them or they see it via text or video—their short-term memory engages, but there is little long-term gain. They can retain the information long enough to pass tests that are administered immediately, but they

[28] "Neuroplasticity and the Brain," www.transforming-child-behavior.com/neuroplasticity.html.

[29] Brenda Patoine, "Applying Insights from the Study of Normal Aging to Solve Dementia," The Dana Foundation, www.dana.org/news/publications/detail.aspx?id=19772.

are unlikely to hold on to it for a long time, and what they do remember is unlikely to significantly change their mental model.

The result of the Thinking Effect is a new or improved mental model. To understand the effects on our mental models, it is helpful to explore some of the latest research in neuroscience to get a better understanding of how the mind works. Let's do that next.

Neural Pathways

Daniel Coyle, the author of *The Talent Code*, believes that talent—from skateboarding to music—is not inherent or "born" into a person; it is created. He describes the importance to the body of myelin, an insulator that surrounds nerve fibers. The more a person practices and fails, then corrects and tries again, the more myelin is built up on neural pathways and the faster the brain receives messages along the neural paths. The increase in myelin causes the learning messages to "stick." Talent, therefore, as Coyle views it, can be developed by repeated practice.

In the same way, employees can practice their thinking skills to build newer and better neural pathways. When these pathways are established, workers can leverage them to generate thoughts in new and changing situations.

The primary actors in the human brain are 100 billion nerve cells, called *neurons*. All of our functions—both conscious and unconscious, both physical and mental—happen as a result of impulses traveling along pathways of coordinated neurons. These pathways are larger or smaller depending on how often the brain uses them.

The brain operates as a whole, but general landmarks can be attributed to the four lobes of the brain. The *occipital lobe*, located at the back of the brain, primarily processes vision. The *parietal lobe*, in the back portion of the upper brain, takes in sensations from all senses but smell. The *temporal lobe*, located on the sides of the brain, is mostly responsible for hearing, emotion, and storing memory. The *frontal lobe*, directly behind the eyes, rules social behavior and personal characteristics, including curiosity, foresight, and capacity to foresee outcomes.

The *prefrontal cortex* within the frontal lobe is responsible for a person's ability to understand and process appropriate actions and consequences of decisions. Interestingly, people do not fully develop this portion of the brain until the late stages of adolescence. As we age, we begin to use the prefrontal cortex more, tapping into a greater well of experience and logic. Through experience, we establish new neural pathways, which equate to new or evolved mental models and habits.

Neural pathways are like trails through the woods. If one person walks on a path one time, the trail will barely be defined and will vanish quickly. But if many people walk the trail, there will be a well-defined path that is easy to see. These defined neural pathways become a comfort zone, a mental model. We tend to fit many situations into these networks and, as a result, we often only explore options that fit our mental model and require little course change from our well-traversed paths. It becomes difficult to veer away from the established practices—even if they no longer apply. This is how habits are formed.

As we all know too well, there are bad habits and there are good habits. They allow us to fall into a "daily routine" and easily manage the massive amounts of stimuli we face every day. However, an unintended consequence of habits is that because they are performed without depth of thought, we miss critical information. We do not pay attention to the minor details of the habits we use.

When an organizational initiative doesn't work out as planned, companies blame inadequate processes, tools, or staff.

But perhaps the real issue is that the organization applied an old habitual strategy to a new situation. An approach that worked in one situation will not always work in the next. Using the same patterns of thinking means people repeatedly come to the same conclusions. Overall, most people's reasoning works fine and gets them by, but it may fail when they are challenged in unique situations. During our simulations, we noted time and again that many participants, even after going through hours of workshops, ended up reverting to old patterns, doing the very things they were told not to do.

The good news is that adults have the aptitude, throughout life, to adapt or change the structural and functional organization of their brains. Simply put, we all have the capacity to replace old habits and create new mental models.

NEURAL LEADERSHIP

Understanding unconscious connections

Have you ever felt really connected with someone, as though you are "on the same wavelength"? There may be a biological explanation for that feeling, which recent studies in neuroscience can help to explain. Our brains are equipped with special neurons called *mirror neurons*. These neurons fire when we see someone else perform an activity we've done before. For example, watching a friend bite into an apple will trigger a similar neurological response in our brain. This can be extended into other areas, such as facial expressions, body language, and tones of voice. Based on someone's action, we may unconsciously experience similar emotions and responses. So, say, for example, during a team meeting, you frown, look distressed, or show confidence. Others will unconsciously process your actions and potentially modify their own behavior to model your behavior. In other words, actions really do speak louder than words.

How We Learn

Another concept to take into consideration when developing learning is the process through which we retain new information. Learners go through various peaks and valleys as they accumulate and implement knowledge. A peak occurs when someone "gets it." The learner develops clarity and can easily retrieve needed information or demonstrate a skill. We see this happen early in organizational training or learning environments.

However, as people learn more, other information pushes the learning out of their short-term memory, and their mental model—or schema—begins to falter. Simple concepts they could easily retrieve become complex, disparate parts that make little or no sense.

Perhaps the best way to explain this is through a story from my personal life. A few years ago, when my son was younger, he was learning to speak Russian. He was doing really well at carrying on simple conversations, and I decided to show off his language skills to some friends who were visiting. I asked my son a few questions in Russian, and he quickly answered every time. I was a proud father—my son was obviously a genius.

A month or so passed, and the same friends came over for a barbecue. Once again, we talked about my son's language abilities, and I bragged that he had now learned conjugations. They wanted to see his progress. We called him over, and to warm him up, I asked him a few simple questions. But this time, he couldn't respond. He tried three times before conceding that the information he had known so well only weeks before had somehow disappeared.

An important concept for organizations to take from this story is that human learning is not linear. An employee may not learn A, then B, and then C (Figure 25). This is especially true for developing *how-to-think* workers.

FIGURE 25 Classic Learning Approach

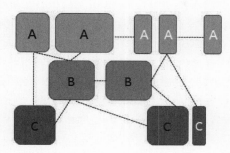

FIGURE 26 Realistic Learning Continuum

Sometimes we learn about A, a bit of B, and then more about A, and then we are ready for C, which may drop us back to understanding different questions about B. The learning continuum in the diagram shown in Figure 26 looks more like an interconnected web than a line.

Workers who are acquiring new ideas or information reach points where they recognize the gaps in their thinking. As a result, there is a temporary period in which their minds "step back" and try to fill those gaps and re-create a new schema. This is what happened to my son the second time I asked him questions. With so much more information flooding his brain (conjugations), his memory struggled to form new answers to old questions.

Dr. Paul Camp, a professor at Georgia Institute of Technology, who for more than thirty years has been studying the ways we learn, best describes this "U-shaped" development curve:

> The notion that performance always improves with time, that the more you learn, the more you know and the more you

know the more you can do, is as close to an accepted law of nature as it is possible to come in education research. It is deeply engrained in all aspects of almost every pedagogical approach. It governs the linear development of ideas in the writing of textbooks and the design of courses and activities. It also governs the evaluation of all of these activities through reliance on pre/post testing. However, as a law, it appears that it may have the same scientific status as the medieval impetus theory. The unspoken notion that you never get worse as you continue to learn has to be called into serious question by the phenomenon of U-shaped development.[30]

We have observed this learning curve in our simulations. Individuals may exhibit confidence in their actions in the first round when the situation is relatively straightforward. Then, as we provide new information and present impacts from previous decisions, those same individuals start to miss simple decisions.

I believe that the new information and results causes them to question what they thought they knew and understood. Initially, they thought that by doing X, then Y would happen. However, when they experienced an entirely different outcome, a gap in their mental model became exposed. During this period, participants search to fill this gap and miss seemingly simple decisions.

If we test the simulation participants in the first hour of the round, it will appear that they "get it." However, as they go through progressive rounds and the situation becomes more complex, they begin to experience cognitive disconnects that separate them from the new material, as well as from the

---

[30] Paul J. Camp, "U-shaped Development of Newtonian Concepts: Implications for Pedagogical Design and Research Practice" (Atlanta: Georgia Tech, 2012), 12.

information they thought they knew. Measurements done at this point often show subpar thinking—not because the participant doesn't get it, but because he is in the middle of constructing a new mental model. The danger within a simulation is that if a participant's gap becomes too big or he exposes too many gaps, he may become deeply frustrated and give up.

It is for this very reason we created new measurement techniques that focus more on providing useful feedback and less on taking snapshots of what participants know at that very moment. Issues with traditional assessment techniques include:

- They don't provide the organization or the simulation participant with any practical feedback data. The most typical "test" is a classic "smile sheet," which is simply a measure of whether the participants liked the course and felt that it met the stated objectives.

- They merely measure an employee's ability to recall information, which doesn't indicate integration of knowledge. These tests may even report misleading information if they are given while the participant is at the low point in her U-shaped learning, where she is reconstructing her mental model.

- They rarely take into account an employee's natural abilities and preferences, and instead focus on the easy-to-measure "snapshot in time."

The goal is not just to test what participants know but also to give them insightful feedback that will help them continue to develop their self-awareness and thinking abilities. In other words, assessments should not be integrated into a course to check whether the participant "got it." Assessments should be integrated within a simulation to surface and illuminate limiting beliefs.

The key then is to provide participants with various forms of feedback and with enough time to incorporate their new thinking and experiences into their newly forming mental models.

As we work with learners in our training programs, we continue to evolve three assessment techniques: cognitive analysis, mode analysis, and behavioral analysis. Each of these techniques captures various data points as the participant progresses through the simulation. This approach reduces the impact of the U-shaped curve as participants' thinking and behavior are charted over time.

Cognitive Analysis examines a simulation participant's application of the Core Abilities and Value Skills. Using Responsive Modeling behind a simulation, we assess participants and give feedback in such areas as:

- *Jumping:* When participants are hesitant, they typically jump between strategies. They hold on to one strategy until another presents some glimpse of hope, and then they shift their energy.

- *Guessing:* When participants are overwhelmed by difficult problems or too much information (noise), they may start guessing in hopes that something may work.

- *Fixating:* When participants don't take the time to understand the big picture, they fixate on solving one problem and unknowingly create new problems.

- *Reacting:* When participants are determined to win or make quick improvements, they make decisions that produce good results in the short term, but create bigger issues in the long term.

- *Filtering:* When individuals or teams make decisions, it becomes apparent which informational elements are used and which are overlooked or not internalized due to lazy thinking.

Mode Analysis investigates which parts of the brain (modes) an employee relies on most, or the personality style she exhibits during difficult situations. Modes define how learners process information, communicate, relate with others, and make decisions. During a simulation, participants adapt to progressively more difficult scenarios, often in relation to other people, requiring them to use a variety of brain functions and personality styles. When participants are placed into difficult situations, their real styles often surface.

Behavioral Analysis looks beyond mode analysis to a participant's reactions to an array of environmental factors. In mode analysis, facilitators give feedback based on preferred styles and how those styles influence team dynamics. A behavioral analysis, by contrast, provides feedback based on the participant's reaction to complications. For example, did the individual melt down when confronted with difficult issues? Did he pull himself together in a thoughtful and constructive way, or did he consciously or subconsciously affect the team? Due to recent innovations, behavior analysis integrated into simulations is now being used in organizations to assess leadership and management capabilities and readiness.

What is helpful about these assessment techniques is that simulation participants are not evaluated on what they know, but on how they think and behave in varying circumstances. The feedback generated from these techniques offers many lenses into employees' habits, strengths, and potential chinks in their armor.

Neural Coding System

We are wired to learn. Yet most people are not great learners. It's not entirely their fault, however. Most of the current methods used for teaching are based on old patterns of thought and have done little to prepare people with the necessary abilities to adapt. The professional instructional design community, which should be at the forefront of innovation, often falls into the familiar "teach to the objective" approach, reducing training to linear chunks of information laced with knowledge checks and bound by pre- and post-assessments in hopes that students will eventually "get it." Recently, many organizations have jumped onto the technology and gamification bandwagon, adding badges, gifting, virtual goods, and leader boards to spruce training up. The good news, for the most part, is that these techniques have improved completion rates. The overall result, however, is still the same: learners may *know* a bit more, but they are not capable of *doing* more.

Applying new technologies or the latest gimmick without applying new design strategies is like applying lipstick to a pig. It's cute, but you still don't want to kiss it. Frankly, as trainers, my colleagues and I found ourselves falling into this same alluring trap. We built the first technology platform optimized for developing *how-to-think* workers, yet we struggled with falling back on habits and using traditional approaches to design simulations. We received rave feedback from participants, but in fact this approach was too shallow. In the end, we realized that we could do a better job at creating environments to allow people to rethink their thinking.

Our underlying driver is that we want to create positive and lasting behavior change that helps workers and, ultimately, organizations perform and treat one another better. More simply put, we want to teach employees to become Value Workers. This only happens if what people learn in the classroom can be applied to different situations.

"Transfer," to the training professional, is the Holy Grail. It refers to how much of what is learned within the learning arena can be applied back to the workplace. We define two levels of transfer:

- *Situational* transfer occurs when learners can apply what they learned to similar situations.
- *Adaptive* transfer occurs when learners can adapt what they have learned to a variety of situations.

There is another dimension to transfer, which we call *capacity*. Capacity correlates with the amount of information that an individual retains and is capable of applying after the learning program. If, for example, an individual can apply many newly learned skills to different situations, then the program is said to have a high adaptive transfer capacity. Part of the goal for training, then, is to increase each learner's capacity for transfer.

Organizations that are trying to get the most out of their employees should note that learning that has a high adaptive transfer capacity is the most desirable for improving each worker's value potential. When it comes to developing *how-to-think* workers, this level of transfer is also imperative.

With this in mind, my colleagues and I have spent a considerable amount of time and resources rethinking traditional principles and evaluating assessment techniques focused on developing *how-to-think* workers. As a result, we created the Neural Coding System (NCS).

Our underlying philosophy for developing the NCS is that the training must cause students to stop and think, reevaluate their mental models, and reach their own insights into how to modify their own thinking or behavior. It must balance learning and practice, leaving students the opportunity to fill gaps and reinforce new skills. It must provide informative and relevant feedback regarding their limiting beliefs within dynamic and complex systems. And, it must be fun and not a waste of time.

Neural coding is a neuroscience-related field concerned with how sensory and other information is represented in the brain by networks of neurons. Neural coding describes the process of neural network formation in the brain in response to a stimulus. The formation of these neural networks determines how people respond to future stimuli. With repetition of any stimuli and response, neural pathways are etched deeply and become the default "programming" for how people behave or respond to similar types of stimuli. As noted earlier, this is the neurological basis for habits and mental models.

The NCS is a design framework that consists of four cognitive conditions that create an optimal learning environment for developing *how-to-think* workers when the conditions exist together. It is not a step-by-step methodology or series of discrete events. Rather, it is an interconnected system of mental conditions that are created through the artful implementation of various design principles. As the image in Figure 27 illustrates, the NCS is more like a funnel. Simulation participants are placed in the middle of new situations that are evolving in response to their decisions and actions. This spiral approach, moving between the various conditions, is critical to engaging workers

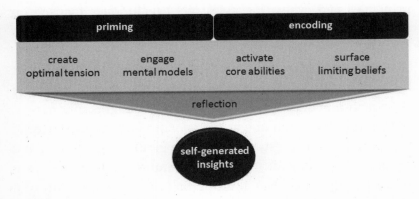

FIGURE 27 Neural Coding System

as they evaluate their mental models and seek to resolve gaps. Through trial and error and reflective dialogue, this approach allows them to work toward that sudden moment of convergence.

It would take an entire book to cover this framework in detail. Instead, I'll share only the primary purpose of each condition by starting with the end in mind: self-generated insights. I've also included a few design principles for each of the conditions. Initially, as you review the principles, you may think, "We already do that in our courses." That may be true, but keep in mind that all these principles incorporate the dynamic responses generated from the simulation. As such, the principles become interconnected, building on the others, to create an emotionally engaging and intellectually rigorous environment to surface limiting beliefs and change mental models. This approach leads to self-generated insights, which is essential to creating the virtuous cycle of the Thinking Effect. Insights create motivation and, in turn, the energy necessary to change mental models.

SELF-GENERATED INSIGHTS

Real learning happens in the moment when a worker combines knowledge and experiences to create something new, such as a new mental model or belief. I can tell you how a system works, but unless you experiment with it, then you're merely sharing my perspective of how I think it works. You have your own knowledge and experiences. If you're going to be effective at making decisions within the system, then you need to construct your own perspective.

When learners work with new material, a small burst of adrenaline is released. This action engages their long-term memory as they build new pathways, or "scaffolding," to help them make decisions. The more people encounter and overcome their own gaps, the more "scaffolding" they build toward retaining and incorporating information that impacts their performance. At this point, real learning begins, and behavior has the potential to change.

Dr. David Rock, cofounder of the NeuroLeadership Institute, and Jeffrey Schwartz, MD, offer a scientific reason for this:

> For insights to be useful, they need to be generated from within, not given to individuals as conclusions. This is true for several reasons. First, people will experience the adrenaline-like rush of insight only if they go through the process of making connections themselves. The moment of insight is well known to be a positive and energizing experience. This rush of energy may be central to facilitating change: It helps fight against the internal (and external) forces trying to keep change from occurring, including the fear response of the amygdala.[31]

That moment—a point at which learners feel a sudden understanding of a previously perplexing issue—is something everyone has experienced. People often call them "insights" or refer to them as "aha" or "eureka" moments. They occur when people sleep, in the middle of a discussion, and in the shower. The Russian scientist Dmitri Mendeleyev went to bed frustrated by a puzzle that eluded him for years: how the atomic weights of the chemical elements could be grouped in a meaningful way. One night, he dreamed of a table where all the elements fell into place. This dream led to the creation of the Periodic Table of the Elements.

Little is known about what occurs in the brain before, during, and after an insight, except that there seems to be spikes of electrical and chemical activity. As my colleagues and I explored and learned more about insights through our

---

[31] David Rock and Jeffrey Schwartz, "The Neuroscience of Leadership," *Strategy+Leadership* 43 (May 2006), www.davidrock.net/files/Rock_&_Schwartz_s&b_43_06207.pdf.

simulation participants, we did observe some common conditions that seem to exist prior to an insight. Here's the kind of typical stream of thought we hear from simulation participants:

> It just happened. I felt that something was wrong, but I could not put my finger on it. It was frustrating, as I believed the answer was right in front of me, but I couldn't see it. I kept trying different ideas and nothing worked. I remember just before it suddenly hit me, I took a break and I was thinking about something else.

There were some common patterns in the participants' responses. First, they tended to switch between emotional and cognitive words as they described their state leading up to the insight. Many participants articulated feelings ranging from anger to peace, while also using phrases such as filling gaps, making connections, and exploring ideas. Another theme people expressed was the realization that what they knew was incomplete or inaccurate. To find answers, they felt they were spiraling between deep thinking and surface-level thinking.

We also observed in team discussions that participants, without actually using these words, surfaced biases, fears, and flawed mental models. For example, when presented with ethical dilemmas, individuals would quickly jump to a conclusion but then realize those conclusions differed among the team. This led to deep discussions about what they believe and why they believe it. Finally, there seemed to be a common pattern that, just before an insight, participants temporarily left the problem and did something else. Whether they were getting a cup of coffee or chatting about a different topic, they gave their brains an opportunity to process and reenergize.

These observations, discussions, and extensive research led us to the four conditions of the NCS system. The first two conditions (*create optimal tension* and *engage mental models*) prime an individual to learn. Priming is an implicit memory effect in which exposure to a stimulus prepares an individual for a later stimulus. The next two conditions (*activate core abilities* and *surface limiting beliefs*) focus on encoding. Neural encoding refers to the connections that are created between stimulus and response; when the brain processes and synthesizes stimuli, neurons spike and connections are made. Underlying the conditions are periods of reflection, to allow the brain to process and reenergize.

Together, the four conditions elicit the mental, biological, and electrical states that create deep learning. It is this integrated strategy that improves a worker's value by strengthening the neural connections so skills are more readily retrievable in novel situations. Let's take a look at the purpose of each condition and a few of the design principles that are used to create the condition.

It's important to note that though the conditions are listed in order, they don't occur in order. Participants flow between them naturally or as a result of the design principles.

CREATE OPTIMAL TENSION

Just as Socrates felt that it was necessary to create "a tension in the mind so that individuals could rise from the bondage of myths and half-truths," learning should cause an internal tension that evokes a desire to learn.

Emotion affects everything we learn. Adults learn most and best when they feel a passion for learning and the learning process. Without that emotional engagement, new lessons fade from memory quickly. When associated with strong emotions, however, new lessons become ingrained and eventually integrated into performance.

This doesn't necessarily mean that one's passion for a subject needs to be positive for true learning to take place. Let's say that a student became familiar with the work of author William Faulkner twenty years ago and that, to this day, he despises Faulkner's writing. If you ask him why, you're apt to get an earful about exactly why he doesn't like Faulkner, complete with references to specific works and examples of the author's style. He's learned a lot, despite the fact that he hates the subject. This is a great example of how emotion—be it positive, negative, or somewhere in between—helps to anchor knowledge in people's minds.

Researchers have long documented the connection between emotional engagement, memory, and learning. When individuals are engaged in a safe but mentally challenging situation, the intensity activates synaptic firing in their brains. There is a physical change in the way their minds process information, which is what helps them retain knowledge and change behavior. Emotional engagement related to learning is so powerful that it possesses the potential to alter the structure of the brain.

When people experience an appropriate level of emotional tension, their brains release hormones to prepare them for learning. During this heightened emotional state, it is more likely that an experience will strengthen synaptic connections for improved retrieval. Advances in neurology over the past twenty-five years have documented how this emotional anchoring of experience in people's memories occurs on chemical, electrical, and cellular levels in the brain. The results are deepened neural connections and evolved mental models.

In a simulation, learning and doing happen simultaneously. For instance, we sometimes ask participants to tackle this issue: How do managers resolve conflicts between the best interests of their employees and customers and the bottom line? Should they choose the short-term benefit to the company or long-term health and viability? What weight should the company's role as neighbor in the community or citizen of the country play in the decision?

Such ethical dilemmas are not merely hypothetical in a simulation. Instead, participants wrestle with conflicting rights and wrongs. In the process, they almost inevitably develop a strong emotional reaction to the struggle, just as they would in the real world.

This range of emotions changes throughout most simulations. In the beginning, for example, employees often tend to feel a certain degree of hesitancy and nervousness simply because they aren't sure what to expect. After this initial trepidation passes and they begin to immerse themselves in the obstacles and challenges of the simulated environment wholeheartedly, participants begin to feel a variety of other emotions, from frustration and anger to elation and excitement.

In Kahneman's book, *Thinking, Fast and Slow*, he observed that participants in a good mood doubled their accuracy on provided tasks while participants in a bad mood struggled even to complete a task. When you are in a good mood, Kahneman explains, you tend to be more intuitive and creative but also less vigilant and more prone to logical errors. This is why finding the optimal tension is so important.

As noted earlier, in our simulations, we do this by adjusting what we call the emotional throttle. As we design a program, we adjust the throttle to create an appropriate amount of excitement and unrest.

The following two design principles give some guidance on setting the emotional throttle:

Make it noisy but not too noisy.

When the amygdala becomes involved, we remember a situation more clearly. Creating some challenge will engage the learners' amygdala, thereby increasing the potential of learning. However, when an overabundance of challenge makes learners feel threatened rather than invigorated by the situation, they tend to shut down. Although world noise and the organizational noise should be added throughout the simulation to assist in creating a realistic storyline, internal noise (e.g., the generation of fear) should be avoided. If the noise becomes excessive, then participants will expend emotional energy by questioning surface-level issues instead of working collaboratively to understand the underlying dynamics of the problem at hand.

Choices are good, but too many choices are bad.

The number of decisions and choices that people need to make are increasing. All of these decisions and choices consume mental and emotional energy. The best way to get learners to miss the big picture is to flood them with too many choices.

The goal, then, is to include just enough noise to trigger participants' reflexive bad habits and just enough choices to make the simulated situation feel real. Too much of either element can defeat the goals of learning and keep participants from seeing the big picture of the system at work.

Other design principles—from gamification and collaboration to acceleration and exploration—also contribute to the emotional richness of a simulated experience. As participants contend with their simulation team members, for example, emotions run high and conflict inevitably occurs. As participants anxiously await feedback about their success in a particular round, self-doubt, anxiety, fear, apprehension, and finally the agony of failure or the joy of success percolate within each of them. Adjusting the throttle is essential to optimize the learning.

These emotional experiences can have lasting effects on decision makers for years to come, because the emotions experienced within a simulation help to ingrain the experiences in participants' minds. Days, weeks, months, and even years later, when those employees encounter real-world situations, the simulated experiences will be more easy for them to recall, providing them with the insights that make a difference.

ENGAGE MENTAL MODELS

Short-term memories take up only a small portion of our brains—an area about the size of a walnut. It follows that as new information is added, old information is pushed out.

Many learning programs fail because they pack too many objectives and too much content into a learner's head without triggering long-term memory. Since short-term memory is limited, more information does not equate with more learning. This is often the case when people are being taught *what to think*. Learners attempt to absorb mounds of information in a short amount of time, and only a small amount is able to stick.

In another common approach, training departments attempt to improve retention and engagement by breaking up content and threading fun activities throughout it. This helps increase the learners' emotional state and the initial feeling that the information was valuable, but the noise of the job inevitably replaces the good feelings and diminishes the perceived value. In our experience, this is what frustrates executives; they know they need training, but they don't believe it will move the needle.

To engage learners, leaders must engage their minds by creating situations that cause them to search their database of mental models to make sense of the situation. It is well established that good decision makers develop rules to help them simplify information processing when faced with complex decisions or problems involving risk and uncertainty.

This idea was first explored in 1963 by Richard Cyert, president of Carnegie Mellon University, and James March, professor of Management at Stanford University, in their book *Models in a Behavioral Theory of the Firm*. More recently, in the bestselling book *Thinking, Fast and Slow*, Daniel Kahneman and Amos Tversky review the evolution. One consistency among all of the reserach is the power and influence that mental models have on people's lives. Simply put, to change behavior requires a change to learners' mental models. Therefore, it is important that learners actively engage their mental models to expose flaws. With long-term memory engaged and a mental model or framework activated, learners incorporate new information in a way that can actually affect their ability to perform.

Here are a couple of design principles we follow when designing programs.

Put it in context whenever possible.

Context warms the brain up as participants search their mental models for similar experiences. When challenged, learners will search their vast database of feelings and experiences to help bring meaning to the current situation. So, if employees are being asked to adopt a new strategy, align with corporate initiatives, or rewrite old organizational beliefs or mental models, then context is critical. They must be challenged in a way that breaks down existing cognitive structures and replaces them with new, more effective models. This occurs best when the context of the learning is rich enough to elicit emotional concern for the outcomes and accurate enough so that the effects of participants' decisions are easily relatable to meaningful outcomes in real life.

On the other hand, if the primary goal is to develop fresh new models or merely have the learners become aware of new patterns of thought, then context is less important and can actually prove to be distracting. For example, if employees are being introduced to new topics like business or financial acumen, then we've found it effective to start them out with a simulation that teaches the basic patterns of thought needed to learn the business and understand the financials. However, for them to internalize and learn to see that their actions contribute to the patterns and behaviors of the organization, we recommend context.

Let them discover it, instead of telling it.

Almost all organizations have some level of a documented strategy. But in most cases, there are only a few people within the business who can articulate how their individual actions influence it. Knowing the strategy is helpful. Developing the strategy is impactful. Knowing how actions and decisions affect the strategy is transformational.

"Strategy" is not something that can be defined as a learning objective by an executive team and proffered to workers the same way they learn passwords and security procedures. Strategy must become part of their *mindset*. So, instead of telling people what the strategy is, a better approach is to have them define it. If there is an already well-designed organizational strategy, then allow the employees to define goals and discover what it will take to achieve them. Either way, participants should monitor their progress and make adjustments as they go. When they discover how their actions—or lack thereof—contribute to a goal or an organizational strategy, they take more personal accountability and responsibility than they would if they were merely told *what to think*.

NEURAL LEADERSHIP

Understanding the need for autonomy

"Telling" not only robs people of their autonomy, it also removes an opportunity for trainers to gain a new perspective. It's difficult to stop telling, however. We learn about telling at a very early age. As children, we're told what to do and what not to do. In school, teachers tell us what to think. Not much changes when we get to the workplace. Lists, processes, and procedures tell us what to do. Bosses tell us what to do. This is all so contrary to what the human brain prefers.

People desire and need autonomy. This need becomes abundantly clear in the teenage years. Even if you're not a parent, you still most likely have heard utterances such as, "I know what I'm doing," "I can do this myself," "I don't need your help," and "I'm an adult." This deep need for autonomy does not go away; it may be suppressed, but it is still very much desired by the brain. Yet, most training programs and educational interactions involve one person telling others what to do or what to think. Being aware that the brain needs autonomy will help you move between the times when telling is appropriate and when inspiring is critical.

ACTIVATE CORE ABILITIES

Cells that fire together wire together. Donald Hebb, considered the father of neuropsychology and neural networks, observed that when simultaneous activation of cells occurs, a deeper synaptic bond is created. In other words, the more the learning is emotionally engaging and educationally rigorous, the more cells fire and the more learning occurs.

The goal for organizational trainers, then, is to create environments in which participants must use visual searching, working memory, and long-term memory to make decisions and evaluate outcomes. This will stimulate brain activity and increase the likelihood that when workers go back to the job and face noise, they will be able to recall and apply these newly attained skills.

An additional benefit to creating a stimulating environment for learning is that it will also overcome the distractions of boredom. Every trainer knows that people get bored easily. There's actually a physiological explanation for it: the process known as "habituation" is a decrease in behavioral response to stimuli after repeated exposure to the same stimulus over time. When the mind goes into that "habitual" state, very little learning can occur. Fewer synapses fire, dopamine is reduced, auto pilot is switched on, and the all-too-familiar daydreaming look overtakes people's faces. Here are a few design principles that help learners activate their Core Abilities.

Less content, more thinking.

More content does not equate to better thinking; nor does it lead to behavior change. When employees come to the realization that what they know is not adequate for the current situation, they become motivated to fill those gaps. If you give learners too much content, they won't have time to internalize the gaps in their mental models. And, if you give them information that is not readily applicable, then there is a risk that they may overlook that information.

Trainers should only give content if the student has earned or requested it. If a student asks a good question or identifies a discrepancy within the data, for example, then trainers should provide additional information. Or, if a student has been placed into a situation, and the simulation or the student reaches the conclusion that he lacks the necessary foundational knowledge, then the trainer should provide relevant content. In designing *how-to-think* solutions, trainers must keep the focus on creating situations that allow for students to discover the effectiveness of their own thinking and evolve it accordingly.

Slightly distort it; don't over-package it.

When information is nicely packaged and presented in a structured manner, learners may not challenge it. As Kahneman explained, we spend most of our life in System 1. System 1 is gullible and biased to believe, so it prefers when information is nicely packaged. System 2, on the other hand, is skeptical and unbelieving but, unfortunately, lazy. So, to kick System 2 into gear, trainers must set up a situation that gives learners a reason to question.

For example, Kahneman observed that when students are presented information in a font type that is difficult to read, System 2 is triggered because the information cannot be easily consumed. To trigger System 2—in other words, the Core Abilities—trainers should not pre-process and regurgitate back to the participants data, teach points, debrief questions, and information set up as bullet points and checklists. Instead, trainers should present this information in such a way to cause participants to stop and think. For example, asking participants to determine the primary and secondary effects based on different courses of actions is one way to prompt System 2 thinking.

NEURAL LEADERSHIP

Understanding the need to reduce losses

An individual's aversion to loss is often greater than the joy she feels from a gain. In other words, the unhappiness someone feels from losing $50 will be greater than the happiness felt from gaining $50. Loss aversion was first proposed by Kahneman and Tversky as an explanation for the endowment effect—the fact that people place a higher value on a thing that they own than on an identical thing that they do not own. This is important to understand because it impacts everything from negotiations to organizational change to brainstorming. For example, when a team goes through a major change, it will be more difficult if they feel as though they are giving things up. This feeling will exist even if the gains will be better over time. Since aversion to loss can even impact areas pertaining to motivation and engagement, it is essential to understand this effect so you can communicate effectively with people who feel they have to give something up.

SURFACE LIMITING BELIEFS

I once met with a Vice President of Operations for a global retail company. We discussed the value of various instruments to surface limiting beliefs, and personality tests came up. He looked at me confidently and said, "I'm an NTFJ, Driver-Analytic, with left brain dominance." I was impressed because I assumed that knowing his style and personality profiles would help make him an excellent manager and motivator. Then I saw him in meetings acting like a buffoon to his employees and peers. As I watched his rude and ultimately inefficient behavior, it became apparent that despite his knowledge of these labels about himself, he possessed only the data points and not real awareness of himself or his relationships with others.

Labels are essentially cognitive shortcuts that make it easier for us to group, identify, and refer to things and people in conversation with others. For example, consider the image that comes to mind when you hear the words, "She's an Analytic." You may think of an individual who is smart, slow to change, and meticulous. You may consider this a positive label, while someone else may think of similar traits and consider "Analytic" to be a negative label. You have each developed similar understandings of the characteristics associated with the labels but different opinions of the label.

Depending on your organization and your role in it, you will jump to varying conclusions when you hear certain labels. For example, if you are an entry-level employee in a large organization and you hear, "He's an executive," you will have a different perspective of what that means than if you are an executive there yourself. Likewise, you may have an entirely different reaction to the words, "She's an executive."

Labels are helpful insofar as they can speed up conversations and help people make sense of situations. That is why assessment instruments are so popular. People can envision a "Driver" or an "Amiable." They understand what being an introvert or extravert means. The labels help individuals bring meaning to things and people. Yet if learners are not aware of their own label associations, this language, like biases, can stunt the growth of their mental models.

We will never do away with common organizational language—nor should we. As Peter Senge pointed out, "You can't live your life without adding meaning or drawing conclusions. It would be an inefficient, tedious way to live."[32] It becomes a determinant when people either live up to the labels or merely write others off because they have assigned a certain label.

My favorite story that demonstrated the insufficiencies of labeling occurred in a leadership simulation. The focus was to help participants discover the underlying dynamics that shaped their organizations so they could lead more effectively. I remember meeting one leader who was exceptionally intelligent. From my understanding, he rose through the ranks as a result of his thinking abilities. During the simulation, he expressed to me that he felt he had hit a glass ceiling and was no longer effective or being considered for any promotions. As I observed him interact with the different simulation teams, it became apparent that he was brushing off certain people. After one of the debrief sessions, I asked what he thought of those individuals' ideas. He looked at me in a puzzled way and said, "I don't know. I did not hear them come up with any ideas." My observations told a different story: most of the people he ignored actually came up with the best ideas in the simulation.

During a later discussion with him, I showed him a simulation report that demonstrated how they did come up with many

---

[32] Peter Senge, *The Fifth Discipline: The Art and Practices of the Learning Organization* (New York: Currency Doubleday, 2006).

good ideas that could have significantly helped the team. Again, he looked puzzled for a moment. Then I saw the light come on and he thoughtfully said, "This was a real eye opener. I labeled each of those people on day one and have since discounted anything they had to say. I simply was not aware of this."

Assessment tools can be extremely useful in helping to surface blind spots and strengths. However, assessments alone are not enough; what is necessary from a neurological point of view is surfacing these knowledge points in the context of real-world issues. In the intensity of a simulation that reflects organizational challenges, real behaviors—those hidden by years of practice—often break through. Then participants begin to internalize how their individual biases are distorting their abilities to truly hear others. This is one of the reasons why reflection underlies all of the conditions.

When trainers set the emotional throttle appropriately, participants in simulations are able to evoke the necessary mental and emotional states for self-reflection. The goal of invoking these conditions and times of self-reflection is to help participants connect their actions to the responses of other participants, as well as to the outcomes within the simulation. Here are a few other design principles to consider when creating the condition for surfacing limiting beliefs:

More dialogue, less talking.

In a simulation environment, a facilitator is there to *facilitate*, not to teach. A facilitator's primary role is to help participants make their own discoveries by asking good questions and answering their questions. This requires that facilitators must hold a unique mindset, accepting that students' takeaways may differ from their own beliefs, but that diversity of thought is what enables individuals and organizations to become exceptional. This happens through effective dialogue.

Decision-making and problem-solving experts often ask my colleagues and me how to teach people to ask good questions— the kind of questions that expand people's minds and make them reconsider their mental models. Good questioning leads to deeper learning. Good questioning also leads to unlearning of limiting beliefs.

Facilitators should model questioning, reflection, and dialogue by asking different types of questions: summary, analysis, hypothesis, and evaluation. *Summary questions* help provide a framework for the situation.

- What is the underlying issue?
- Who is involved?
- When does the issue occur?

Analysis questions go a bit deeper by asking what factors are contributing to the issue.

- How is it happening?
- What are the reasons for it happening?
- What conditions exist when it happens?

Hypothesis questions, or what we call *mental simulations*, ask "what if?"

- What if we changed this condition?
- If we add a new condition to the situation, how does that change what happens?

Finally, *evaluation questions* help determine if the new conditions are good or bad.

It is important to understand that there is a difference between getting students to ask these questions and allowing students to experience these questions. Unless facilitators foster an environment in which the students can examine how their analysis was incomplete, how adding a condition changes the outcome, or how they can assess outcomes, they won't internalize the experience or surface limiting beliefs.

COLLABORATE, *DON'T* JUST COMMUNICATE

To make sense of the world, people need to label and form beliefs and assumptions about what they hear, see, feel, smell, and taste. When people meet someone new, they tend to judge whether that person is like them or not. If the answer is yes, they may be more open to what the other person has to say. If the answer is no, then their biases may work a bit harder to confirm their newly formed beliefs and assumptions about the other person. Frankly, neither of these reactions is good.

Getting people to communicate about their feelings, issues, or differences is not enough to subdue the biases. So, what works? We have found that when people of diverse backgrounds come together around a shared problem, they somehow find common ground and unite by creating a shared vision. We call this *collaboration*, because each person earnestly seeks to understand another's view in an effort to solve a shared problem. Honestly, I'm not sure how and why this happens, but I've seen it happen time and time again in simulations. We challenge a newly formed team of culturally or educationally diverse backgrounds with a big, audacious problem. They focus, they collaborate, and they typically are giving high-fives by the end of the simulation.

In the next few years, I believe we will see many advances in training and how we learn. Over the last several years, numerous books and new studies have come out exploring the brain's capacity to learn and adapt. New technologies that are driven by voice and gesture recognition are gaining momentum. Recently, I've been playing with some new technology from NeuroSky that monitors my brain waves as brain teasers are presented to me on my phone. It tells me when I'm focused and when I'm drifting off. It even has a mode for teaching me how to relax. All this for only $80! This type of technology was only found in universities and research labs more than five years ago.

I foresee that in the near future, many organizations will institute learning labs. These labs will be places where a range of stakeholders solve systemic problems collaboratively; where partners identify and resolve issues along the supply chain; and where organizations vet new ideas, business models, and strategies. With each advancement, trainers will need to rethink learning—not just fixating on how to incorporate new technology, but identifying how to optimize learning and behavioral change. Time and global reach will continue to grow as challenges, so the impact of training will need to be greater. It's an exciting time to see how neuroscience, computer science, and behavioral science are converging and shaping how, when, and where organizations learn.

Convergence of Technology and Methodologies

As my colleagues and I developed training that could allow organizations to help their workers learn how to think, we set out to create new technologies and methodologies for developing Value Workers. Our goal was to develop new ways of thinking that could be applied to dynamic and complex situations. Along the way, we were excited to assist with many organizations' most pressing challenges. Let's look at what happened when we were asked to assist with the development of the critical and system-thinking abilities of the US Air Force students of the Air Command and Staff College.

GENERATING INSIGHT BY IMMERSION

The US Air Force Air Command and Staff College (ACSC) prepares field-grade officers, from major to colonel, around the world to command air, space, and cyberspace power in complex multinational operations. The officers' earlier professional military education experiences focused on tactical and operational skills, but ACSC prepares them to take on increasingly strategic decision-making responsibilities.

Until recently, the online version of the ACSC curriculum included heavy volumes of reading material and a multiple-choice exam administered at a controlled testing center. This was an effective way to measure knowledge and comprehension skill levels, but it did not address the specific strategic and critical-thinking goals of the program.

The Dean of Distance Learning, Dr. Bart Kessler, wanted to raise the bar of performance for his students by delivering a more engaging and intellectually challenging learning experience. But he had constraints: 10,000 students with varying mental models and biases regarding national security, no instructor-to-student ratio, and some students without access to the Internet.

Dr. Kessler came to us, and we created the National Security Decision Making (NSDM) simulation for ACSC. Within the simulation, students are assigned a role as a national security adviser and have to successfully complete multiple national security–related missions. (See Figure 28.)

The goal is not to train students to "win"; rather, it is about getting military leaders to stop and think about unintended consequences. Using the Neural Coding System, the simulation provides the following:

FIGURE 28 Main Screen from the NSDM Sim

- *Tension:* Each mission is set in a different global hotspot encompassing both tactical and strategic-level problems. Though the simulation has thirty-plus hours of content, it is only provided to students as they need or request it. World and agency issues are streamed into the various missions to add realism and noise.

- *Mental Models:* As students are dropped into new missions, they have to rely on their own knowledge and experiences to assess the situation and determine an appropriate course of action. As they identify gaps in their mental models, they can access foundational content. If the simulation determines that a student is struggling, then it will direct students to additional content.

- *Core Abilities and Value Skills:* To complete a mission, students need to analyze information and make recommendations. Students then predict the likelihood that a particular course of action will satisfy national objectives while accounting for the reactions of regional and global stakeholders. Students have the opportunity to influence global security and so begin to think more strategically about how daily decisions affect larger global issues. The students must balance competing agendas, long- and short-term results, and desired outcomes.

- *Surface Self-Limiting Beliefs or Behaviors:* The simulation is equipped with a Confidence-Based Assessment (CBA) engine that assesses an individual's ability to apply particular subject matter effectively. CBAs measure whether a person is overconfident or hesitant in particular areas. In addition, various instruments are incorporated to provide students with insights into how their belief systems differ from or are similar to other interested parties or stakeholders.

- *Self-Generated Insights:* Instead of telling participants *what to think*, the simulation gives them the opportunity to learn *how to think* by reflecting on their own decisions and actions within each mission. Missions leverage different design techniques, such as cause-and-effect, stated objective, and what-if analysis to provide an environment that allows for discovery. Those techniques, along with a strong real-world storyline and Socratic and systemic impact feedback, allow participants the opportunity to generate their own insights.

This realistic, immersive format offered insights that challenged the officers' mental models by helping them learn to think critically, creatively, and systemically about policy making, security decisions, and international relations. This is particularly important, considering the complexity of the global military presence around the world and the speed at which events are unfolding.

NEURAL LEADERSHIP

Understanding the value of a vision

People really don't appreciate feedback, but they do appreciate a better vision. Too often, leaders approach feedback much the same way they approach solving business problems. They break it into parts, determine which part is broken, and fix it. This method may work to identify deficiencies in processes or across the supply chain, but applying it to humans is a big mistake. In fact, applying any process to people is a big mistake.

Humans are the most complex of complex systems. Relying on a multistep process to give and receive feedback can be done, but it creates a lot of unnecessary damage along the way. The reason feedback processes rarely provide the desired outcomes is because they can cause a reaction similar to the well-known fight-or-flight response to a threat. Recent discoveries in neuroscience suggest that when people hear feedback associated with a problem, they search their memories and uncover associated negative emotions. Consciously or unconsciously, these emotions invoke a defense mechanism that triggers biases and erects walls. The well-intentioned—and most likely needed—feedback does not get fully processed or internalized, so little change arises.

When it comes to feedback, the most brain-friendly approach is to have people arrive at their own solutions. As a leader, you can help create a vision by asking questions that allow people to generate their own insights into what behaviors are needed to achieve the vision. Be careful not to be manipulative or leading, as this will produce an unconscious threat. Rather, drop any expectations and take an active interest in the process of helping others define their own vision.

The Other Part of Our Journey

Designing new technologies and methodologies was paramount to the mission my colleagues and I set before us: creating great leaders and value workers. Yet these technologies and methodologies were not enough to sustain our mission. We realized that if we wanted to help people get to the value-spanning phase on the Value Continuum, we needed to go deeper. And, whatever we did needed to be something that could be done outside a structured training program.

This was not an easy task, because the real world is, well, real. In a training program, participants have some level of control. However, in the real world, there are so many competing factors requesting their emotional and mental energy. It is tough for people to get the feedback from others and from the systems in which they work. It is tough to make time to think. It is tough breaking through all the mental noise to focus on the problems at hand. To help people sustain the valuable insights they received within the simulation, my colleagues and I were led to develop the concepts of the Core Thinking Practices. In the final part of this book, you'll learn more.

PART IV

· · · · · · · · · · · · · · · · · ·

Beyond Training

A human being . . . experiences himself, his thoughts and
feelings, as something separated from the rest—a kind
of optical delusion of his consciousness. This delusion is a
kind of prison for us, restricting us to our personal desires
and to affection for a few persons nearest us. Our task
must be to free ourselves from this prison by widening
our circles of compassion to embrace all living creatures
and the whole of nature in its beauty.

—Albert Einstein

IN AN IDEAL WORLD, we would all prefer to take the smooth road
of the Value Continuum path, as shown in the graph in Figure
29. Because of the reality of the world in which we live, however,
a more likely path looks like the wavy line in Figure 29, which
represents value and lies between the Value Continuum line
and the Cost line. Most of us oscillate up and down like this.
We swing back and forth between those times when we feel on
top and are maintaining the big picture and those times when
we're looking up from the valleys, where we feel overlooked and
are reacting to issues. The challenge, then, is to reduce the time

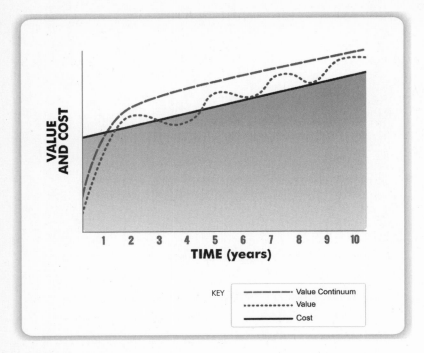

FIGURE 29 The Value Continuum

spent in the valleys. This is done by learning *how to think* and by becoming aware of the derailers and the impact they have on our thinking, attitude, and performance.

This may seem straightforward in the context of a simulation, but what about after participants return to their day-to-day work environments? Maintaining a *how-to-think* mindset amidst the familiarity of the work world is difficult. Most of this book, up to this point, has focused on creating *how-to-think* workers within simulations, so now let's focus on how to sustain that level of thinking beyond training—throughout life.

In 1983, Howard Gardner's *Frames of Mind: The Theory of Multiple Intelligences* introduced the idea of *interpersonal* intelligence (the capacity to understand intentions, motivations, and desires of other people) and *intrapersonal* intelligence (the capacity to understand yourself and your own fears and motivations).[33] Gardner's theory suggested that intelligence is not only made up of the Core Abilities but also includes emotions and the ability to recognize your fears, beliefs, and biases in the thinking process.

This is why my colleagues and I feel that we can't just teach people *how to think*. Trainers need to also equip people with the abilities that allow them to adapt emotionally to new situations. This conclusion led to the development of the Core Thinking Practices (the Practices). The Practices provide a framework for applying the Core Abilities while, at the same time, they help learners to uncover limiting beliefs.

Core Thinking Practices

The Practices are a way for employees and teams to discuss simple and complex systems that shape and drive organizations. They are not meant to be followed as a process or applied as a procedure. Instead, the Practices consist of a common language and patterns, guideposts, and tools that all lead to one thing: generation of thoughtful questions. The language gives diverse organizational teams a way to describe a situation. The patterns serve as a lens to examine typical business dynamics, enabling teams to identify causes and forecast possible outcomes. The guideposts help teams stop from unwittingly contributing to the very problems that they're trying to solve. The tools surface biases and incomplete mental models that are often at the root of endless nonproductive discussions or failed efforts.

---

[33] Howard Gardner, *Frames of Mind: The Theory of Multiple Intelligences* (New York: Basic Books, 2011).

Each Practice begins with the word *seek*. We chose this word thoughtfully and with purpose, because it conveys the effort required to enact the Practices. Learners must not give in to the plausible, visible factors, but rather search deeper to understand the underlying dynamics. The Practices trigger critical-, creative-, and systems-thinking abilities to help learners think more systemically about their decisions and actions. The table shown in Figure 30 presents the mental shift that occurs as a result of using the Practices.

A word of caution: Some of the concepts may seem like commonsense ideas, so it's easy to overlook the nuances. Keep in mind, though, that even commonsense ideas require thought to understand and effort to put into practice. Some Practices will certainly resonate with teams, while others may take time. Encourage teams to stick with them and use the Practices to help make decisions and deal with complex situations. As long as these Practices provoke deeper thinking and help teams make sense of ideas and situations that don't seem to make sense, they have served their purpose.

Practice	Mental Shift
Seek to understand the big picture.	Move from a linear mindset to a systemic viewpoint.
Seek to understand the underlying behavior.	Move from fixating on an event to observing patterns and structures.
Seek systemic change.	Move from short-term fixes to long-term initiatives.
Seek to surface limiting beliefs.	Move from jumping to conclusions to suspending judgment.
Seek to evolve a shared vision.	Move from boundaries around beliefs to a borderless mindset.

FIGURE 30 Core Thinking Practices and the Mental Shift They Create

Each Practice is meant to help teams shed light on a situation by reframing it from different perspectives. Notice the cycle: As teams learn about the structure, they will gain insight into the underlying behavior. This insight leads them to a more systemic view and helps surface limiting beliefs. As teams expose limiting beliefs, they start to see more of the underlying behaviors at play. This continuous process of moving between the Practices will improve thinking and increase the value workers bring to the organization.

AWARENESS

Self-awareness and awareness of others is foundational to the Core Thinking Practices. To move between the Practices, it is essential to expose the derailers and understand the perspectives of other people.

The renowned psychotherapist Carl Rogers wrote a famous book published in 1961 entitled *On Becoming a Person*. The book has had an enormous influence on defining healthy relationships. Rogers's approach to others is called "Unconditional Positive Regard."

"Unconditional Positive Regard" means to relate to another person without judgment, to listen in a manner that causes the other person to feel heard, to accept fully what might be weaknesses of another, and to provide an open, supportive presence. While we would all welcome this quality of relationship, it is difficult to achieve because it is dependent on an individual's ability to acknowledge her own manufactured beliefs. This is done through self-awareness.

Valuing others begins with looking in the mirror at ourselves. This introspective look raises a number of questions.

- Are we clear on our deepest personal values?
- Is our behavior consistent or congruent with our values?
- How do we deal with internal value conflicts?
- Do we make decisions that are consistent with what we value?
- Are we emotionally honest in our reactions with others?
- To what degree are we open to people who are different from ourselves?

These questions are all helpful in the process of uncovering those artificial barriers that are constructed throughout projects or even during the course of the day.

Now, this may seem like we are moving into "touchy feely" territory here, but I assure you that we are not. Let's return back to the Value Continuum model and the value path. This path is typically fraught with peaks and valleys. A shift that is due to external factors, such as policy or market changes, and that is compounded by the derailers, may cause employees to struggle to find ways to add value. Obviously, this is not a good thing for the employees or the organization. The goal, then, is to recover quickly. Merely improving employees' skills and thinking abilities may not be enough, however.

Oftentimes, there are deeper reasons or competing priorities that need to be uncovered. Robert Kegan, Professor of Adult Learning and Professional Development at Harvard University, and Lisa Laskow Lahey, Research Director of the Change Leadership Group at the Harvard University Graduate School of Business, found that ". . . as [people] hold a sincere commitment to change, many people are unwittingly applying productive energy toward a hidden competing commitment."[34]

[34] Robert Kegan and Lisa Laskow Lahey, "The Real Reason People Won't Change" (Boston: Harvard Business Review, November 2001), 86.

Kegan and Lahey describe a case regarding a talented software engineer named John, who ". . . was a big believer in open communication and valued close working relationships, yet his caustic sense of humor consistently kept colleagues at a distance." John was provided consistent feedback about this issue, ". . . but time after time, [he] reverted to his old patterns." As it happened, "John was a person of color working as part of an otherwise all-white executive team. . . . Underneath it all, John believed that if he became too well integrated with the team, it would threaten his sense of loyalty to his own racial group." In John's case, his shift toward subpar value was the result of both an external circumstance and something personally deeper. And, unless he became aware of the deeper issue, his value would be diminished. This is why all of the tools we've developed or incorporated examine individual and organizational beliefs in the context of business systems. The Practices have been specifically crafted to address these deeper dynamics.

Earlier chapters have already covered a few of the tools my colleagues and I use to develop individual and team awareness. We use both responsive modeling and impact mapping to help people develop a big-picture perspective while seeking to understand the underlying dynamics. For example, we did the impact map exercise described in Part I with a group of engineers who, as a result of the process, discovered they all had different mental models of how advancement worked in their group and how success was measured. They even discovered that these different beliefs inadvertently created some of the very problems with which they were most frustrated. It was gratifying when they finally got on the same page, and it didn't take them long to gain agreement. This is partially due to the fact that the impact map forces the participants to focus on the system and its behavior instead of trying to find something or someone to blame.

We've also successfully used the behavior-over-time graphs, also discussed in Part I, to help individuals track key indicators over time. There is nothing easier than having a discussion with someone who has been plotting the peaks and valleys of an issue over time. When it comes time to discuss the underlying behaviors causing the fluctuations, few emotions are involved, and attention can be directed toward uncovering manufactured beliefs or real contributors (e.g., ineffective policy or process).

We will keep coming back to the importance of developing a deeper awareness as we discuss additional tools. For now, let's review some of the common language and business patterns teams can use to describe the underlying dynamics of a system.

COMMON LANGUAGE AND PATTERNS

The language of Core Thinking Practices is already part of your vocabulary. You have likely heard the concepts as parables, advice, or cultural stories.

One example is the following well-known parable, called "The Blind Men and the Elephant." The story originated in India and has been modified and used by all major religions. In the various versions of the tale, an unidentified creature has entered the land and several blind men, who are considered experts at deduction, are sent to determine what it is. Each blind man approaches the creature and describes the unknown animal according to what he feels. The descriptions of the elephant include a wall (the side), a spear (the tusk), a snake (the trunk), a tree (the knee), and a brush (tip of the tail).

> And so these men of Indostan, disputed loud and long
> Each in his own opinion, exceeding stiff and strong
> Though each was partly in the right, they all were in the wrong

This parable exemplifies one of the Core Thinking Practices: Seek to Understand the Underlying Structure. It shows how individual perceptions can distort group beliefs and illustrates the limitations and interconnectedness of team members' views.

As the world continues to become more interconnected, having a shared language to explain dynamic situations will be essential for people of diverse backgrounds and cultures to work together to solve problems. Scholar Benjamin Lee Whorf noted that language shapes thoughts and emotions, determining one's perception of reality.[35] Add cultural and societal beliefs to the mix, and perception becomes even more divergent. Successful collaboration is largely due to an individual's or team's ability to explain problems without blaming others.

This is why systems language is so powerful. The language provides a way for people of varying backgrounds to discuss and explore systems. Organizational issues such as planning, anticipating limits to growth, and implementing sustainable changes are already difficult when everyone speaks the same language. Add diverse backgrounds, and the only way to create a shared vision is to rely less on spoken language and leverage systems language to explain common and complex business patterns.

The following sections provide a brief overview of some of the language typically used to describe systems. As you read through these examples, I encourage you to think of how the patterns and stories play out in your organization.

Archetypes

Archetypes represent common organizational behavior patterns seen in all organizations of all sizes. The archetypes help

[35] Benjamin Lee Whorf, "Science and Linguistics," *MIT's Technology Review*, April 1940, http://web.mit.edu/allanmc/OldFiles/www/whorf.scienceandlinguistics .pdf.

learners form questions and test assumptions for each of the Practices. For instance, learners who are trying to understand the big picture can use the archetypes to provide visual representations to help them create an impact map. For learners who are exploring system behavior, they provide examples of how the patterns behave. They can help learners understand Responsive Models and identify leverage points—those small adjustments individuals can make within a system that change how the system behaves.

One of the first mentions of system archetypes was in Peter Senge's book *The Fifth Discipline: The Art and Practice of the Learning Organization*. Senge outlined five disciplines essential to any organization dedicated to growing and learning. The fifth discipline Senge identified is systems thinking, which he called the key to integrating the other disciplines. To explain the power of systems thinking, he created the "eleven laws of the fifth discipline," which are also known as system archetypes. Figure 31 offers a brief description of some especially useful archetypes.

Managers, leaders, and consultants can apply archetypes both as a diagnostic tool to uncover patterns of behavior within an organization or as a planning tool to help test assumptions and anticipate potential problems. When this is done in the context of an organization, the employees, who are often closer to the problem, gain the language and tools necessary to uncover the underlying issues while separating personal and organizational biases. In doing so, they're more likely to identify high leverage points that are better for the people and functional areas in which they work.

Leverage Points

A leverage point is a small adjustment an employee makes within the system that changes how the system behaves. Leverage points

Archetype	Description
Need to Balance Process with Delay	As a business acts toward a goal, the teams making the decisions are often operating from delayed feedback. If employees are not aware of the delay, the business may continue to devote more resources than necessary and end up with a surplus.
	Other dangerous mental models that affect balancing process with delay include:
	• "Let's generate more data, more metrics, and more processes to compensate for the delays."
	• "Let's add more resources to mitigate the delay."
	• "Let's change the process."
Limits to Growth	Growth cannot continue unabated. As an organization pushes forward, at some point something will push back.
	Typical mental models that fail to recognize limits of growth include:
	• "We're too big, too smart, too far ahead of other organizations."
	• "We've grown 20 percent annually for a decade. Why shouldn't we expect to continue to grow?"
Eroding Goals	When a goal seems unattainable, individuals or organizations respond by lowering the bar. For example, a manager realizes that a team continues to fall short of its quarterly goals. Instead of assessing why they're missing goals, the manager simply restates the goal by lowering the target.
	There are recognizable indicators of eroding goals:
	• "This goal was set by a clueless executive, so it's not likely to be attainable."
	• "I know the goal will be adjusted down, so I'm not going to invest too much time or energy in it."
	• "We don't have time to do everything right this time, so let's just lower the goal until the next project."

FIGURE 31 Common System Archetypes

(Continues)

Archetype	Description
Escalation	Two competing organizations perceive their success as dependent on the failure of the other. Each side acts more aggressively toward its own advantage until there is so much enmity built up on both sides that both find dwindling profits. Typical mental models that contribute to escalation include: • "Do whatever it takes to sustain a competitive advantage." • "We must get the lead at all costs." • "That's our job—we are supposed to compete."
Fixes that Fail	A short-term solution to a symptom of a problem may have unforeseen long-term consequences that need even more of the same short-term fix. Common mental models related to fixes that fail are: • "It's a simple problem, so don't spend too much time on the solution." • "Implement a quick fix for now, and we will deal with any issues that come from it as they arise." • "The fix didn't work because we didn't apply it thoroughly." • "Fix it now, or I may lose my job [or the project may fail, or the team will fall apart, etc.]." • "It looks like we are going to fall short on revenue this quarter, so let's offer a discount to win more business."
Tragedy of the Commons	Individuals take advantage of the shared resource for their own profit without sufficient concern for the limitations of the resource. As the resource diminishes, there is no appropriate feedback to raise concern. The outcome is overuse of the resource to a point that it becomes unavailable to everyone.

FIGURE 31 Common System Archetypes   *(Continued)*

Archetype	Description
Tragedy of the Commons (Cont.)	Typical mental models leading to tragedy of the commons include: • "There are more than enough resources for everyone." • "It's not my responsibility to monitor or limit use of the resource." • "It costs too much money to implement appropriate triggers to inform us when a resource is being overused." • "We don't have the time right now to explore alternative resources."

FIGURE 31 Common System Archetypes   *(Continued)*

represent the various levers that are pulled to change things systemically. A low leverage point means a small action yields little change. A high leverage point means a small action yields a larger change in behavior throughout the system.

The goal is for employees to identify high leverage points that positively change the behavior of the system in which they're working. This is typically done by making small changes across the system and adjusting appropriately as they receive feedback from the system. Take, for example, cultural changes. An organization's culture determines how employees work, their investment in the organization, the responsibility they feel, and even their personal interactions. Yet, most changes are made at the surface level—the things that can be seen and observed. For example, providing and summarizing cultural surveys, implementing social media tools, or instituting monthly team or divisional communications are all important but don't address the underlying system. Culture is a complex system, and attempting to change it quickly by applying hasty fixes often yields emotionally strenuous consequences.

As Senge pointed out:

> Often leverage follows the principle of economy of means: where the best results come not from large-scale efforts but from small well-focused actions. Our non-systematic ways of thinking are so damaging specifically because they consistently lead us to focus on low leverage changes: we focus on symptoms where the stress is greatest. We repair or ameliorate the symptoms. But such efforts only make matters better in the short run, at best, and worse in the long run.[36]

To find high leverage points, employees must examine each problem from a variety of different angles and from differing points of view. This is extremely important when dealing with complex business systems. The more workers can step back and embrace the larger system, the easier it will be to find a simple solution that makes the biggest difference. It is important for solution seekers to forget about the individual parts and how complex they are and instead focus on the interactions between the parts. Understanding these common patterns helps people find simple solutions.

One of the main strengths of the archetypes is that they provide a common language for simple behaviors within complex systems. They help problem solvers keep the focus on the interactions between the parts and, in doing so, they lead to the revelation of simple solutions to big problems.

Take, for example, this hypothetical but common scenario:

> Everyone was excited! The executive team presented a powerful vision for a new product—the super widget. The super widget was

[36] Peter Senge, *The Fifth Discipline: The Art and Practices of the Learning Organization* (New York: Currency Doubleday, 2006).

amazing, destined to spur a real product revolution that certainly would set the company apart from its competition.

Energized and enthusiastic, employees went back to their desks to begin developing their strategies to bring the super widget to market. After the strategies were defined, project managers worked weeks to create masterful project plans outlining exactly how implementation of the strategy would work and how each team would contribute to the implementation.

Three months into the project, the executive team checked in with their employees. "On target and on budget," the teams reported. Six months into the project, the leaders checked in again. "We're on target and on budget!"

Executives were happy with the updates, and they began to generate buzz in the market.

Then the bad news came: they were going down the path of the death march. With only forty-five days left until the planned release of the super widget, team leaders said, "We're way off target and over budget and we still need to deliver on time."

I remember one organization that experienced these "death marches" on almost every project. Somewhere along the line, the team lost track of the system, leading to major issues. Realizing the impact this was having on morale and ultimately on their inability to scale, the company sought to understand the underlying dynamics. Using the Practices, they learned about the system and the influence it was having on the visible factors, such as morale, breakdowns in communications, and ineffective processes.

First, they noticed that team leads were hoarding resources and inadvertently causing other leads to hold on to their resources until they were needed. This problem was not easily noticed because the impacts did not surface for months. The delays in the system made it difficult to pinpoint the cause, but by the time it was figured out, a great problem existed.

Further exacerbating the problem was the fact that the teams were staffed with exceptional people who created a "healthy" competitive environment. Again, at the surface, what is wrong with a little healthy competition between teams? However, a common pattern—escalation—began to emerge across the organization, in which teams over-engineered their projects, causing the need for heroic effort.

Furthermore, the hoarding of resources caused another common pattern—tragedy of the commons. So, as new projects started up, there was not enough of the right resources to staff them adequately. The leadership responded, just as many leaders would, by adding more meetings. Their intention was good: fix the problem by improving communication and processes. The open communication was helpful, but the problem did not go away. Rather, it created an initial feeling of progress but ultimately complicated matters.

The tangled web created by these competing challenges took time to unravel, but the team took it one layer at a time. First, they created an impact map of the problem so they could clearly see the common patterns. Using the map, they examined the various feedback loops and the delayed effects, which gave them insight into the underlying behavior of the system. In the next layer, they unpacked the organizational and individual biases. As you can imagine, the group uncovered many biases at work, from how each team lead was framing their problem to justify their actions, to redirecting blame, to creating collusive relationships.

Finally, they arrived at three common underlying issues to which they all contributed: (1) gold plating (over-engineering their part of the project, which created delays elsewhere), (2) starting from a blank slate (because they are high performers, it was more fun to reinvent than reuse), and (3) lack of convergence (they moved into different phases of the project before everyone on the team was ready or understood why). The awareness of these three underlying behaviors allowed the team to create a shared vision—that is, they created a picture of the future that they could all aspire to and evaluate their individual actions against. This individual accountability helped them implement the needed improvements in communication and processes.

GUIDEPOSTS

The guideposts help teams stop unwittingly contributing to the very problems that they're trying to solve. As teams are generating questions, the guideposts serve as reminders of some of the thought patterns that lead to linear thinking. Figure 32 outlines a few suggested guideposts for teams and leaders to consider as they apply each of the Practices.

Practice	Guideposts
Seek to understand the big picture.	• **Change perspectives.** To understand how a dynamic system actually works, look at the system from a variety of different angles and from differing points of view.
	• **Avoid doing one big thing.** Fixating on one thing may improve that one thing, but most likely it will create multiple other unintended issues. Typically, it is best to make incremental changes across the system.
	• **Avoid easy targets.** Be very suspicious of any proposal to alter or eliminate an apparently "useless" part of the system.
	• **Watch for stabilization.** As with any living system, organizational systems seek ways to stabilize. Maintain an *active* bigger picture perspective because it's only a matter of time before the system changes.

FIGURE 32 Core Thinking Practice Guideposts *(Continues)*

Practice	Guideposts
Seek to understand the underlying behavior.	• **Anticipate delays.** When actions are taken within a complex, dynamic system, the outcome of the action may not be seen for some time. If the delays are not understood, the organization may continue to devote more resources than necessary and end up in a bigger mess.
	• **Identify the archetypes.** To help create a shared vision, the various archetypes at play in order to provide everyone with a common language. This places the focus on understanding the system behavior and not on people or language barriers.
	• **Analyze feedback loops.** When actions are taken, the rate at which a change can be observed is based on the established feedback loops. Feedback loops can accelerate change or decelerate change—an essential behavior to be aware of when growing a healthy organization.
Seek systemic change.	• **Avoid obvious solutions.** If someone tries to change something in the direct, obvious way, the system is going to treat those efforts like any other outside influence and do its best to neutralize them. Leaders should understand that genuine solutions require careful thought to create effects on the whole system.
	• **Discuss effects.** Causality is often considered but rarely explored. Great leaders go below the waterline to understand what is causing an issue to rise to the top.
	• **Identify leverage points.** Not all systems will offer the same leverage points. Identify what these are.
	• **Understand and then speak.** When people begin a conversation, they naturally start at the surface level. It is important for leaders to go deeper before jumping to a conclusion.

FIGURE 32 Core Thinking Practice Guideposts   *(Continued)*

Practice	Guideposts
Seek systemic change. (Cont.)	• **Fail small and often.** Dynamic systems imply that things are constantly changing over time. Initially, it will be difficult to identify a high leverage point. Don't let "perfect" get in the way of "good;" rather, they should make small changes and be prepared to adjust.
	• **Run mental simulations.** There are a lot of problems in organizations, and there is a sense of accomplishment when something is taken off the list—though only for the short term. Explore possible short- and long-term outcomes to avoid the pitfalls that drain both the emotional and intellectual energy from the organization.
Seek to surface limiting beliefs.	• **Don't become overly confident.** When people are sure of something, they usually don't look elsewhere for something new that may provide insightful guidance. Leaders need to accept that things are changing too quickly and are too complex and they need the council of many.
	• **Don't manage thought and emotions away.** Under pressure, there is a tendency to apply too many processes in an effort to control the system. As things become emotional, there is a need to establish control. Instead of managing thought away and controlling emotions, leaders should encourage people to share their limiting beliefs.
	• **Be aware of deeply rooted habits.** Everyone is shaped by their own biases and mental models. The mental models that people have developed over the years influence how they respond toward, act to, treat, and view the world. Leaders must help their teams identify deeply rooted habits and how to alter them if necessary.

FIGURE 32 Core Thinking Practice Guideposts *(Continued)*

Practice	Guideposts
Seek to evolve a shared vision.	• **Be honest.** Wishful thinking, seeking information that only confirms an existing bias, or framing for positive response will only propagate limits. Leaders must seek to create a shared vision by avoiding the need to spin information for their own gain or protection. • **Share common language.** Leaders must ensure that everyone shares the same language when discussing systemic problems. • **Evolve good system behavior.** Good leaders blame the system, not the people. Blame is not an effective strategy to bring about lasting change. • **Set a vision.** A vision should evolve, not dissolve. Leaders must set a vision and then collaborate to evolve the vision as more data become known. Good leaders are bold, fail fast, and adapt quickly.

FIGURE 32 Core Thinking Practice Guideposts   *(Continued)*

Remember that these are merely suggestions to consider and not hard-and-fast rules. The Practices are meant to trigger the Core Abilities and help people better apply the Value Skills. One more reminder: the Practices are fluid; there are no perfect starting or ending points. Learners will flow from one to the next as questions and insights enter their minds.

ASKING GOOD QUESTIONS

The ultimate goal of the Practices is to generate good questions.

I believe not all questions are good. The art of asking good questions is often discussed, but it is poorly understood and applied. This is unfortunate because good questions open people's minds and bad questions close them. Yes, there are bad questions.

Each brain is a searchable database, designed to store information, find and retrieve answers to questions, and solve problems. But the answers generated by the brain depend on the quality of the questions that are asked. Better questions make the brain search deeper, pushing past immediate emotional or surface-level responses and searching for solutions instead of excuses.

It is through good questions that learners uncover the system's structure and begin to understand its behavior. Good questions poke below the surface of an idea and expose potential pitfalls, improving the quality of eventual decisions. Good questions shed light on each individual's own biases and the biases of others, helping learners create a deeper awareness. Good questions challenge perceptions and expose flawed thinking. Good questions help ensure that the right problem is being solved. However, it is often the case that, while trying to uncover the real problem, people tend to jump to conclusions about what they hear at the surface level and fail to go deeper.

Jumping to Conclusions

To make sure teams are solving the right problem, they must learn to avoid jumping to conclusions. To make sense of the world, people have to process information quickly, and this means they need to make quick judgments. Sometimes, their very safety depends on quick judgments. However, people often apply this same level of reactive thinking to situations that require a more deliberate and reflective way of thinking. If teams apply reactive thinking to complex situations, then most of their energy will be expended on untangling the emotional web created by quick judgments.

We recently worked with a professional consulting company. The team lead, Veronica, described a reactive situation she had experienced:

I was sure that my team was trying to sabotage me. They knew if this project went well I would get promoted. The week prior to our final release was rough. Communication between the account manager and the client were strenuous. The client contacted me directly and said he needed one more change implemented. I pulled the team together on a Thursday afternoon and told them about the change request. I felt like the entire team thought it was my fault. I could not believe they would think that, because I've been working so hard to keep the project on track. I suggested a few solutions, but received little support. I was bristling with indignation at this point, so I told them all that they needed to work the weekend to get the change done.

By jumping to conclusions, Veronica overlooked the fact that this last-minute change request was new to her team and they needed time to process it. Similarly, the team overlooked the fact that Veronica was equally frustrated with the last-minute change and the client, and they failed to notice that she was embarrassed to ask for their help—especially over the weekend. The truth of the matter is that the team would have been more than happy to work the weekend for Veronica because they were well aware that she had worked a number of weekends so they would not have to. That's a lot of emotional energy wasted—a waste that equates to a decrease in productivity and team morale.

NEURAL LEADERSHIP

Understanding the need for energy

The need for energy is so widely understood but yet so poorly attended to. We all know how the lack of sleep erodes our ability to focus. We feel the impacts that multitasking has on our energy and performance. We know that surviving from one caffeinated drink to another may get us through the day, but it will inevitably leave us feeling depleted by the evening. Yet, even though we know how important energy is to quality thinking, most people tend to do little about it.

I believe this lack of commitment to maintaining our energy is largely due to cultural expectations. Working, being at your desk, and producing is rewarded. Leaving our desks for a brief walk, or having lunch without scanning emails on the phone, or carving out time during the day for exercise—these behaviors are not rewarded. Yet from a brain perspective, pushing hard without taking a break will reduce performance and may lead to health problems.

As a leader, breaking ingrained habits or cultural expectations may be the key to creating a higher-performing team. Encouraging people to take walks throughout the day or to take breaks during long meetings or lengthy periods of concentration will help them reenergize and improve productivity. Also, instead of offering workers cups of coffee, provide them with some positive recognition. Their brains will release dopamine, which is a natural energy booster. Refer to "Thinking Energy" in the Appendix for other suggestions.

The simple fact is that we are all like Veronica. We receive information, quickly filter it, interpret what it means to us, formulate a conclusion, and act on it. This process can take seconds or days or percolate over an extended period of time. If the wrong information is interpreted and acted upon, it can be detrimental to our careers and our personal lives. And, worse, it can shield needed information that initiates and fosters behavioral change.

A few years ago, as part of our rethinking thinking challenge, we embarked on what has become an amazing journey of helping business people develop a higher sense of awareness. We started by studying the work of Chris Argyris, a business theorist and Professor Emeritus at Harvard Business School, to gain a deeper understanding of how people jump to conclusions.

Steps	What's Happening?
Observable data	Information and data are being gathered.
Selected data	Data are filtered, and only select pieces that resonate with our reality are retained.
Assumptions	Because the data cannot be neatly organized, assumptions or generalizations are applied.
Conclusions	Based on the interpreted facts and data, conclusions are drawn.
Beliefs	Based on the conclusions, new beliefs are added, and old ones are modified.
Action	The newly formed belief is turned into action.

FIGURE 33 Ladder of Inference

Argyris created the "Ladder of Inference," which describes the thinking process that a person goes through, from the initial fact to a decision or action.[37] This tool is exceptionally useful for catching yourself when you turn information into action without much thought.

Each step of the ladder defines a person's mental state, in which data are being processed, organized, and formulated into action. The first step starts with the reality and facts we receive through our senses. After the information is received, it moves through the steps shown in Figure 33.

The problem is that very few people stop to reflect on these steps. This is primarily due to the fact that the brain goes through these steps in the blink of an eye. That is why awareness is so important—people must learn to catch themselves and be willing to step back and reflect on their conclusions and assumptions.

---

[37] Peter Senge, *The Fifth Discipline: The Art and Practices of the Learning Organization* (New York: Currency Doubleday, 2006).

For example, Veronica could have had a more productive team meeting if she had realized that her team needed time to process the situation: why did the client call you, why now, why is this change so important, what is the change, what are our options? Instead, Veronica observed them withdrawing as she explained the change and immediately concluded that they didn't appreciate how hard she had been working and the situation she had been placed in.

The image in Figure 34 illustrates the steps of the Ladder of Inference that Veronica quickly climbed during the meeting. Starting from the bottom and working upward, you can see how Veronica went from observing their behavior to making a conclusion to reacting to the situation.

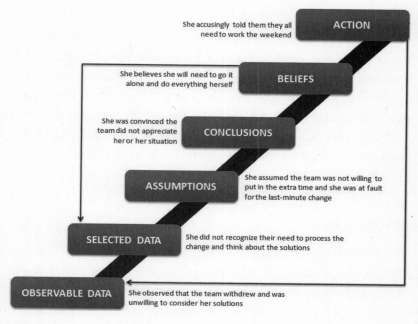

She accusingly told them they all need to work the weekend — **ACTION**

She believes she will need to go it alone and do everything herself — **BELIEFS**

She was convinced the team did not appreciate her or her situation — **CONCLUSIONS**

ASSUMPTIONS — She assumed the team was not willing to put in the extra time and she was at fault for the last-minute change

SELECTED DATA — She did not recognize their need to process the change and think about the solutions

OBSERVABLE DATA — She observed that the team withdrew and was unwilling to consider her solutions

FIGURE 34 Veronica's Ladder of Inference

Without awareness, it is also easy to get trapped in the recursive loops. The first loop is from Beliefs to Selected Data. This loop implies that Veronica has a choice of what data she selects and what data she disregards. At this point, Veronica believes she is going it alone, so she is missing the fact that the team needs time to process. The second loop goes from Actions down to Observable Data. This loop implies that the actions that Veronica takes will most likely shape the situation to create similar data. In this case, Veronica told her team to work the weekend, which made them withdraw even more.

An alternative approach would be for Veronica to question her own assumptions and conclusions. For example, she may ask what data she selected and why she selected them. This may lead her to explore what deeper underlying dynamics are at play that she can't easily observe. For example, Veronica's team really wanted her to be successful and recognized how hard she had been working.

It is not difficult for learners to know when they're caught in a recursive loop, or vicious cycle, because it quickly becomes an emotional and cognitive energy drain. Being aware of this drain and having the willingness to break out of the loops is important to applying the Practices. As learners generate questions, they will surface information and data quickly. The challenge is for learners to avoid jumping to conclusions based on the observable data.

Example Questions

The example questions shown in Figure 35 are meant to expose system-level data and surface assumptions and conclusions about the data. Each question in the table is listed with the Practice it addresses. This is by no means a complete list; rather,

Practice	Questions
Seek to understand the big picture.	• What is the overall need?
	• How do you measure success?
	• What problem are you trying to solve (speed, quality, cost, revenue, profit)?
	• What are the key factors at work (internal and external)?
	• Who are the key people involved?
Seek to understand the underlying behavior.	• What are the important tradeoffs or balance points, and which factors are being balanced?
	• What can happen from a bad decision, and how long does it take for the results to show up?
	• How long does it take for good decisions to improve business results?
	• Are any vicious or virtuous cycles apparent? Under what conditions?
Seek systemic change.	• What can be controlled?
	• What types of decisions can have the most positive effect on the business?
	• Which actions can have long-term effects— positive or negative—and what are the effects in the short term?
	• Which actions can produce quick results, and what is the long-term impact of them?
Seek to surface limiting beliefs.	• Do people have different opinions about the problems or possible solutions? What are the differences in their assumptions? Under what conditions would they all be correct?
	• What are the common traps that people can fall into here? What creates the trap? How do they get trapped?

FIGURE 35 Example Questions   *(Continues)*

Practice	Questions
Seek to evolve a shared vision.	• What problems are they trying to solve? Does everyone involved have the same end goals—the same definitions of what success looks like? If not, what are the differences?
	• Do people understand how their actions contribute to the vision?
	• Is the team willing to evolve the vision as new information is uncovered?

FIGURE 35 Example Questions   (Continued)

it is meant to further your understanding of each of the Practices and how each question can be used to examine different parts of a system. I suggest thinking about additional questions as you go through the examples. It's also important to that for the example questions to be useful, each would need to be generated within the particular context of the situation you are addressing.

For example, my colleagues and I are currently working with a global manufacturing and distribution company that is growing too fast. To help the employees generate their own understanding of the situation, we created a simulation that allows participants to explore the limits of the organization and the limits of their own thinking by "testing" its structure and exposing deeply rooted organizational beliefs.

We asked the participants what each of them could do to reduce the influence of these limits. This got the teams thinking. They asked questions such as these: If the limiter is a critical set of resources, can new products or services that are less reliant on these resources be emphasized? What are the limits beyond those that are obvious to us today? How will we know we are pushing up against these limits early enough that it is possible to throttle back on growth before harming the business?

As long as we guided the participants back to keeping a big-picture mindset, the dialogue and ideas kept flowing. One individual, inspired by the discussion, jumped to a flip chart and drew a series of brick walls, one behind the other. He explained to the group that if they could start to think more systemically about this issue, they might not have to always be in reactionary mode. He continued by pointing to the first brick wall and said, "If we can explore potential challenges behind each wall, then it may get us thinking about what we need to do now to prepare. For example, we're experiencing limits to internal resources now. Next, it may be supplier limits, then thinning markets, and then a new competitor."

Throughout the next few days, the team moved between exploring potential barriers to discussing changes to the current structure. They not only generated legitimate ideas for the organization, but they also united around a shared vision of figuring out what they needed to do collectively to prepare for growth.

The Practices helped take the lessons from the simulation to the realities of the workplace. In time, through repetition, the participants got better at spotting the patterns, trends, and structures in the workplace. And that is what it is all about: How to increase the transfer of skills back to the workplace in a variety of situations. This leads us back to the Thinking Effect.

The Thinking Effect

An organization's success in the coming years will largely be due to the quality of the people it hires and grows. This is by no means a new concept; people have always been critical parts of an organization's success. But now success is going to depend on more than whether individuals can achieve the tasks in their job description. Today's workers must also demonstrate an ability to lead themselves through the shifting priorities and opportunities. Therefore, as we've argued here, the most pressing educational need today is developing each employee's ability to learn outside the classroom.

No matter how much traditional training companies put into workers, the extent to which these workers add value depends on how well they develop their thinking abilities. Like any skill, effective thinking becomes stale without effort to sustain it. Providing constant training exercises is impractical, and even if it were not, workers must be the ones to motivate themselves toward continuous improvement. This continuous motivation comes from their ability to assess gaps and limitations and their willingness to address these deficiencies. It comes from their understanding of the Thinking Effect.

Throughout this book, I've presented the abilities, skills, and practices necessary to create Value Workers. The Thinking Effect describes the underlying changes that occur to mental models as a result of the virtuous cycle created by the application of the Core Abilities and Value Skills. It is this effect that improves the application of all other skills.

No matter what skills workers are learning, managers, leaders, and consultants should ensure that the Core Abilities serve as the focal point throughout the learning process. All learning should lead to improved decision making and problem solving in a collaborative manner. This new way of thinking and learning creates Value Workers.

Despite the increasing need for refined, multifaceted thinking, most people do not continually evolve their mental models. In the spirit of system thinking, if an organization is the sum of the thoughts of its people, then the highest leverage point for changing an organization is to change how its people think.

A key dependency of the Thinking Effect is that organizations provide the initial push—they get the mental ball rolling, if you will. Achieving that initial push is not easy, however. We don't need Newton's first law of motion to surmise that when workers' mental model boots are stuck in concrete, the company will have a hard time gaining momentum. On the other hand, if organizations can help workers break from traditional ways of perceiving and interpreting the world, then they can build a powerful momentum.

Figure 36 demonstrates how it all comes together to form the Thinking Effect.

Guided by awareness, the Core Thinking Practices set in motion an effect that shapes mental models. Starting with the Core Abilities and moving upward, the Practices trigger the Abilities as systems-level questions probe the situation to form a big-picture perspective. The information gathered and insights generated from the Practices inform the Value Skills. As decisions are made, the Practices are once again employed to determine the effectiveness of the decisions and expose additional information about the underlying system. These data points are fed back to the Abilities for deeper evaluation and reflection, further refining mental models. The result of this cycle is

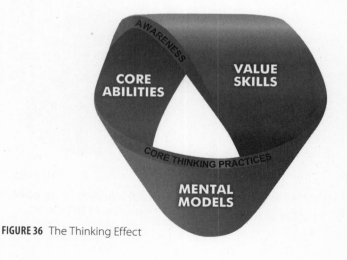

FIGURE 36 The Thinking Effect

improved transfer of learned skills. Most importantly, this effect occurs outside structured training events.

Here's how the Thinking Effect is applied to leadership. In the diagram in Figure 37, the largest outer circle represents the domain of leadership knowledge, skills, and behaviors. However, while people may know about all competency skills and appreciate how important those skills are to becoming good leaders, their ability to apply those skills will be limited to their mental models and capacity to apply the Core Abilities.

Each of the gradient circles in Figure 37 represents an expansion of the mental models and Core Abilities as a result of the Thinking Effect. Each time leaders evolve their mental models and refine their Core Abilities, they further improve their capacity to apply other leadership skills and, in turn, increase value as a leader.

This new way of thinking and learning is also necessary to create Value Workers.

FIGURE 37 The Thinking Effect
Applied to Leadership

Domain of leadership, knowledge, skills, and behaviors

CREATING GREAT LEADERS AND VALUE WORKERS

The path on the Value Continuum is a lifetime journey. Along the way, there are those moments in which you can see how your value as a leader has helped others or shaped an organization. As your value increases, your need for external recognition decreases. You recognize that you are part of something bigger. As you move up the Value Continuum, it becomes less about the money, though that will come, and more about the positive difference that you make to the system and to those working within it. Value Workers who think critically, creatively, and systemically about their decisions and actions create something much more sustainable and rewarding when they focus on improving their own thinking and the behavior of the systems in which they live, work, and play.

Imagine the world fifty years from now. The information overload we suffer from today is still there, but the Value Workers of the next several decades have broken the linear reductionist way of thinking with a new way of thinking. By developing their Core Abilities, they have come to understand the underlying dynamics of the problems they solve and decisions they make. They are able to anticipate unintended consequences, suspend their judgment, and explore different perspectives. They recognize places where they are wasting their time, others' time, and organizational resources. They feel compelled to fix a recurring problem instead of adding another layer of processes and short-term fixes. They take accountability for their decisions because they realize that they're part of something bigger. They do not easily jump to conclusions, redirect responsibility, or accept information at face value. Their thinking pours over organizational walls into the communities they serve. They have learned to harness the Core Thinking Practices to surface limiting beliefs and hone their skills. They have developed awareness to quiet the noise and create understanding.

Call to Action

It is my hope that this book will give us all a vision for the future by outlining what needs to be done right now. I also hope that you're as excited as I am about being part of changing the approach to organizational thinking.

We all benefit when each of us is willing to share, wants to be challenged, and is interested in exploring new approaches to thinking together. I offer a call to action. Anyone interested in being part of an effort to rethink thinking in order to create great leaders and value workers should e-mail me at mvaughan@ thethinkingeffect.com. I will organize a consortium so we can share, learn, and grow together.

. . . .

Common Types of Simulations

THE FOLLOWING ARE THE MOST COMMON types of training simulations, which can be used for a variety of purposes. It is helpful to understand these general categories when selecting a simulation for a specific need.

Remember, technology is only half the answer. The other half is methodology. Be wary of simulations that use traditional technologies and instructional design processes. They consume subject matter expert time and drive indirect costs way up. Be sure whatever solution you choose can be delivered in the classroom, via the Internet, and leverages new devices. This is critical to maximizing your investment. You'll want to build once and be able to deploy in multiple formats. This includes the ability to restructure the simulation into different formats, such as offering it for a one-day session, spanning the sim over a few weeks, or integrating it as reinforcement to another program. Avoid the "black box" simulations that require you to use their facilitators within the classroom. I call these "feel good" simulations. Since the experience and emotional engagement is far superior to traditional training, everyone leaves feeling good about the experience. In other words, the learning is boxed but the ongoing costs are not.

Participant Role	Common Simulation Types
Active	***Desktop (or Tabletop) Simulations*** are typically used in emergency response situations. Teams work together to quickly make decisions as a crisis continues to unfold. These simulations are best geared to training emergency response teams and executives.
Active	***Role Simulations*** create an environment in which learners take on a role, which evolves based on other participants' reactions and responses to various situations. These simulations are best geared toward discovering a participant's strengths and weaknesses. They also can be used to introduce new ideas.
Active	***Decision (Branching) Trees*** take a participant down a set of predetermined paths. In such simulations, a participant often is confronted with various situations and is asked to select the best decision or course of action. Based on the choice made, the simulation then branches to another situation that builds upon the previous one.
Active	***Spreadsheet Simulations*** are used to model simple business concepts. Users typically input numeric data that are processed by a series of formulas and macros. These simulations are best used for developing basic business and financial acumen.
Active	***Goal-Directed Simulations*** are similar to branching simulations, but they also include a predefined goal that the participant tries to achieve. Games often fall into this category, providing motivation, structure, and a goal to create a supportive environment for learning. Goal-directed simulations are best suited for teaching specific skills.

Participant Role	Common Simulation Types
Observational	**Discrete Simulations** are usually used to model the effects that certain variables have on populations, systems, or sets of processes. In a discrete simulation, entities change state based on how a learner responds to various events. The passing of time does not have a direct effect. Orders arriving, products being developed, and products being shipped are examples of discrete events. Discrete simulations tend to provide more detail than continuous simulation designs regarding the workings of a system.
Active & Observational	**Responsive Simulations** create an environment in which a participant takes on a role and is required to address many different situations and issues in parallel. Responsive simulations integrate role-based simulations with discrete and continuous simulations. They do not have any predetermined paths. Rather, the simulation evolves or responds to the learner's thinking across many interconnected decisions. Responsive simulations tend to be the best solutions to real-world business issues, such as running a business, taking a product to market, and understanding the impacts that operations, sales, marketing, and finance have on one another. They also develop a participant's systems and critical-thinking skills.

Common Simulation Engines

The following are the most common types of simulation engines that are used to process participant inputs and provide feedback. There are many derivatives of each engine type, and different vendors may assign different names to each engine. Focus on the characteristics of each engine when you choose a simulation.

Spreadsheet Engines most often fall into a category called *discrete simulation models*. Discrete simulations involve individual actions that are not connected; each segment is simply a single event in time or in a series of isolated events. For example, changing one value within a spreadsheet will create tangible changes on the rest of the sheet, but using spreadsheet calculations to display complex system changes (various interdependent relationships that evolve from internal and external inputs) is much more complicated. Even if it could be done, maintaining it and expanding would not be feasible.

Decision Tree Engines are perfect for organizations that need to impart a skill that requires a great deal of repetition and has a known set of possible outcomes. Evaluating performance is a relatively easy task with a simple decision tree engine simulation, because each choice can be labeled as "Best," "OK," or "Inadequate." The computer can assign scores to the different labels and determine how an employee did overall.

To illustrate, examine the tree diagram to the left. The top node symbolizes a question with three choices. When the participant selects a choice, she branches to the next level. The process continues until the participant achieves the goal or reaches a dead end.

Decision tree engine models are limited in that they cannot determine how events occur in relation to other events. For example, a decision made in one division of a company within a decision tree engine will have no bearing on the other divisions of the company (even though, in reality, different divisions affect one another all the time).

Because of this, decision tree engines are best suited for use with rule-based and goal-driven simulations, where there is a specific goal that must be reached. A simulation that teaches employees what happens in a stable, controlled environment

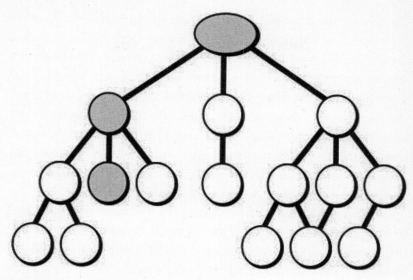

FIGURE 38 Decision Tree

when different chemicals are mixed together, for example, is a good use of a decision tree model. Not many outside factors would come into play as several chemicals are added together to produce one reaction.

Decision engines have some significant drawbacks for other applications. Each level of the tree becomes exponentially more difficult to develop. In addition, decision engines can often feel contrived, causing many participants to spend more time trying to "game" the simulation than learning from it.

State Engines are more complex than simple decision engines. Instead of merely allowing learners to navigate from one predetermined path to another, state engines allow learners to jump from one decision point to entirely different outcomes (or states). Within a state engine, every decision or movement, however minute, has the potential to influence the overall outcome of the simulation. State models offer a far more realistic experience than simple decision trees or spreadsheets because they are not constrained to predetermined paths. Instead, depending on the changes made in the current state (inputs a learner provides, external variables, and data generated by the model), the learner jumps to a different state or level. This gives the simulation a more realistic feel, because the results of the same behaviors in real life can change from minute to minute. Similar to the decision tree engine, state engines are costly to build due to the number of rules and triggers that need to be implemented in order to give it a realistic feel.

Responsive Engines (Models) are the most powerful and best for modeling real-world situations, business dynamics, and behaviors. A responsive engine evaluates multiple decisions made by the participant and combines them with external conditions to produce both task and system feedback.

Task feedback relates to a decision or action that a participant or team performs on a specific task. *System feedback* provides insights into how the decisions and actions made at the task level affect the entire system.

These engines are best suited for "real-world," complex situations that involve many factors and deal with randomness and uncertainty on a large scale.

When modeling the dynamics and causal connections of a business, a responsive engine is the best solution. Due to advances in technology, the responsive model is the most cost effective of all the different engines.

Thinking Energy

What does a person's physical health have to do with the Thinking Effect? Actually, quite a lot. Endurance and the quality of our thinking are directly connected to the foods we eat. Therefore, the modern phenomena of sedentary lifestyles and sugar-filled junk food become the final barrier that holds an organization back from reaching its potential.

Healthy bodies support healthy minds, which in turn work harder and better in the workplace. Poor nutrition, on the other hand, hinders brain development and functioning. Dr. Alan Logan, author of *The Brain Diet: The Connection Between Nutrition, Mental Health, and Intelligence*, provides extensive research demonstrating that poor nutrition not only leads to cardiovascular disease and cancer, but also medical conditions such as depression, anxiety, multiple sclerosis, Parkinson's and Alzheimer's diseases, migraine headaches, ADHD, and more.[38]

Art Kramer, at the University of Illinois, found that simple aerobic exercise improves episodic memory and executive functions by about 20 percent. In a study of adult development, Kramer found that if a seventy-year-old consistently exercised for one year, such as walking a few miles each day, his brain would have the connective potential of a thirty-year-old. It's difficult not to find research that supports healthy eating and simple aerobic exercise in improving brain development and ultimately performance. Exercise has been shown to correlate to the production of new synapses, an increased production of neurotransmitters, and improvement in both short- and long-term memory.

Fast food, fast gratification, and fast pain management have become barriers to productivity. Fast saves time, but it doesn't save energy. A greasy meal will not provide the same amount of energy or concentration as a balanced meal.

Similarly, a "right now" workplace culture that expects immediate access and quick answers will not provide employees with the energy or stamina to endure over the long term.

---

[38] Alan Logan, *The Brain Diet: The Connection Between Nutrition, Mental Health, and Intelligence* (Nashville: Cumberland House Publishing, 2006).

We predict that the successful organization of the future will be more engaged with its employees' energy levels and will support initiatives that make workers alert and productive. The barrier of unhealthiness is becoming too great to ignore.

On average, people who exercise and eat healthier foods tend to be more resilient. They can work longer hours more productively, and when confronted with the daily noise, they have the extra energy to respond thoughtfully.

Sony Pictures recently instituted The Energy Project, a management program that focused not on time clocked but on their employees' four core needs: emotional, mental, spiritual significance, and physical (which included nutrition, sleep, and exercise). Starting from the executive leadership down, Sony employees were encouraged to find ways to increase their own energy supply by the choices they made and to build habits that would support their long-term stamina.

The suggested new rituals, as Sony Pictures called them, were simple: taking an afternoon walk to get a mental break, shutting down e-mail while working on important tasks to avoid interruptions, or banning e-mail during meetings. The company established a time frame, from 8 A.M. to 8 P.M., Monday through Friday, when workers would be expected to return e-mail. Nights and weekends belonged to the employees, and contact during those times was for emergencies only. Here are the results:

> To date, the reaction to this program has been overwhelmingly positive. Eighty-eight percent of participants say it has made them focused and productive. More than 90 percent say it has helped them bring more energy to work every day. Eighty-four percent say they feel better able to manage their job's demands and are more engaged at work. Sony leaders believe that these changes have helped boost the company's

performance. Despite the recession, Sony Pictures had its most profitable year in 2009.[39]

The good news is that our brains do have a capability to restore themselves, even all the way through our adulthood. So there is plenty of time to see the results of crushing this last barrier and addressing a need for healthy living.

The Future of Learning

New technologies, advances in neuroscience, and a better understanding of how we learn will continue to shape learning and development. Sims will play a key part in this, enabling new ways of learning and thinking about problems, often collaboratively. Below are some key new technologies and methodologies.

CROWDSOURCING SIMULATIONS

Crowdsourcing is gaining momentum. Crowdsourcing is the process of outsourcing tasks to a distributed and asynchronous population. Over the past few years, there have been numerous cases demonstrating the power of crowdsourcing to solve complex problems. In the fall of 2011, online gamers cracked the structure of an enzyme in an AIDS-like virus that had been stumping scientists for years. Using a game program called Foldit, which combines collaborative and competitive aspects, gamers identified the crystal structure of monomeric protease

---

[39] Tony Schwartz, "The Productivity Paradox: How Sony Pictures Gets More Out of People by Demanding Less," *Harvard Business Review*, June 2010, http://hbr.org/2010/06/the-productivity-paradox-how-sony-pictures-gets-more-out-of-people-by-demanding-less/ar/1.

enzyme in just three weeks. The journal *Nature Structural &*
Molecular Biology responded by crediting gamers and researchers as collaborators.[40]

Now this new way of thinking is providing a new framework
for identifying the causes of many diseases and developing drugs
to block them. Crowdsourcing has helped solve problems related
to DNA sequencing and new ways to preserve food. Similarly,
as we have discussed, system dynamics–based simulations have
proven to be the most effective way to develop higher-order
thinking skills. New simulations are combining gaming, crowdsourcing, and system dynamics simulations together into a massive multiplayer framework (MMF) to create the next-generation
advanced distributed learning environment.

In the MMF, participants work both individually as well as
collaboratively to solve organization problems or crack into markets. Using the mobile device or browser, participants broadcast
tasks of a larger issue to the community. The crowd is rewarded
for viable solutions that are used by the broadcaster or deemed
viable by the crowd. The system dynamics models help participants expand their thinking, leading to better questions, which
in turn lead to more viable options. All broadcasts and responses
are tracked to build knowledge bases that are used for decision
support.

INTELLIGENT SYSTEMS—SMART MODELS

Smart models with "minds of their own" will become essential to creating more realistic simulations. Models will not only
be based on mathematical conditions but will also evolve and

---

[40] "Online Gamers Crack AIDS Enzyme Puzzle," *The Economic Times*, September 20, 2011, http://economictimes.indiatimes.com/tech/internet/online-gamers-
crack-aids-enzyme-puzzle/articleshow/10047807.cms.

change as they interact with the participants. In other words, the learners will not be the only ones learning.

As individuals or teams run simulated businesses, a competitive business run by the computer will respond with the tactics of a formidable opponent. Learning from its mistakes and observing the actions of the human players, the computer will derive new ideas and attempt risky business decisions.

At any point in time, a snapshot of the model and human decisions can be captured for analysis. From a learning perspective, employees can look at various decisions and their impacts, compared with the responses of the market and smart model. Essentially, the snapshots capture the best and worst practices, or the learners' intellectual capital.

Aside from offering educational and intellectual repository benefits, smart models will offer another benefit to organizations—the ability to play out "what-if" scenarios at the time of need. Imagine that your organization has a new product and your research points to Europe as a high-growth market. Instead of depending on heroic effort and lots of money to test the opportunity in the real world, the various scenarios could be played out in a simulation. The program would give insight regarding potential investments in marketing and advertising, possible operational impacts on production and distribution, and, of course, estimated returns on investments.

REAL-TIME, REAL-WORLD INPUT

Today's simulations, for the most part, incorporate fictional input. Participants progressing through a current-generation simulation might receive a "news alert" informing them that a hurricane has destroyed the company's manufacturing facilities in a particular region. Or a "press release" might introduce a competitor's latest product. These simulated events and communications mimic what *might* happen in the real world, yet they are not real.

The advent of real-time, real-world input, by contrast, will allow next-generation simulations to receive communication from the real world in real time, and then seamlessly incorporate it into participants' learning experiences. If CNN.com issues a morning report that an earthquake in Europe has destroyed businesses, including several factories that the participants' simulated organization owns, this information would be input into the simulation automatically in real time, creating a lifelike microcosm of the real world that forces participants to contend with the same challenges they would face on the job.

BUSINESS-TO-BUSINESS SIMULATIONS

In the future, watch for business-to-business simulations that allow organizations from different but interdependent industries to train their employees together. While a tire manufacturer trains its employees on one simulation, for example, an automotive company might train its workers on a different, but connected, experiential learning solution.

This capability will allow the two simulations to interact with each other in such a way that the actions of one company affect the other, just as they would in real life. Too many tires produced? Tire prices likely will fall, and the auto manufacturer will benefit. Conversely, if there is a sudden car output shortage because a major earthquake destroyed one of the auto manufacturer's plants, tires would have to be rerouted to avoid overstocking.

Using business-to-business simulations will allow employees not only to have the opportunity to interact with other industries, just as they would while on the job, but also to better see and understand the complexities and challenges inherent to working within interdependent industries.

MOBILE DECISION SUPPORT

Another rapidly growing area for simulations is in the area of online and mobile solutions specifically designed to solve organizations' problems. These new simulations leverage gaming concepts and technology as new research shows that gamers are expert problem solvers and collaborators—the direct result of game success relying on creativity and cooperation with other players.

With the advent of smaller computer hardware and portable systems, "decision support simulations" will become available via handheld devices.

Imagine, for example, taking a break from a high-stakes bargaining session and inputting new data into your cell phone, then instructing it to compute the most likely of outcomes, as well as what your best choices are for changing those outcomes if they are not what you want them to be.

That may be a bit of a stretch, but small models to help you think through scenarios and prompt you with thought-provoking questions are not too far off.

INTELLIGENT AGENTS

The next big improvement for simulations will come in the form of Agents, also called Software Agents or Intelligent Agents. Simply put, an Agent is an independent program that will plug into a simulation environment—where it, in turn, would interact with other Agents already present and with the learner, and evolve according to those interactions. An Agent controls its own actions, not its surrounding virtual environment. This means that for every situation, an infinite number of Agents could be plugged in to customize the learning for each user's individual needs.

Agents are complex and possess human-like characteristics in terms of how they act and respond to certain scenarios; the computers develop preferences similar to a human's arbitrary likes and dislikes. Agents also are capable of changing characteristics over time according to learners' interactions with them.

Imagine working at the customer-service desk of a real-world retail store. On the front line, you never know what type of person is going to approach you next: what his problem or issue, if any, will be; how he will handle the problem; how he will act toward you; and so forth. A simulation with a virtual customer-service desk featuring many Agents would function in much the same way.

Several Agents might be placed in the same virtual environment. Suddenly, a simulated one-on-one business meeting becomes a conference. Not only do the Agents interact with the learner, but they also interact with one another. This makes for the most realistic of learning environments, because the Agents create "relationships" with one another and with the learner.

Glossary

. . . .

Archetypes: Archetypes represent common organizational behavior patterns seen in all organizations of all sizes. The archetypes help form questions and test assumptions for each of the Core Thinking Practices. Archetypes can be applied both as a diagnostic tool to uncover patterns of behavior within an organization or as a planning tool to help test assumptions and anticipate potential problems.

Artificial Intelligence (AI): The field of AI aims to study and design intelligent technology.

Artificial Neural Network: This field attempts to model how the human brain learns through repetition and reinforcement. Similar to how our brains work, an artificial neural network learns from experience, not from programming.

Assessment Techniques: Cognitive analysis, mode analysis, and behavioral analysis.

Behavioral Analysis: An assessment technique, behavioral analysis provides feedback based on the learner's reaction to complications. For example, did the individual melt down when confronted with difficult issues? Did he pull himself together in a thoughtful and constructive way, or did he consciously or subconsciously affect the team?

Bias: A derailer that distorts the information we receive and interpret.

Choice: A derailer that impacts our ability to learn. In an effort to provide consumers with freedom of choice, the business community has created an unintended consequence—there are too many choices, and this inadvertently replaces the liberating feeling of freedom of choice with the burden of selection.

Cognitive Analysis: An assessment technique, cognitive analysis examines an individual's application of the Core Abilities and Value Skills.

Collaboration: A Value Skill, collaboration focuses on the identification of biases and flawed mental models that hinder the progress toward a shared vision. At the core of collaboration is a collective determination to strive for something greater than any individual can achieve alone. It requires a willingness to share and learn. Effective collaboration is not just about getting others to agree; it resides in the ability of the collaborators to surface and discuss the underlying systems behind the problem. When done right, teams that work collaboratively can leverage resources more responsibly, solve problems more thoughtfully, and find new ways to do things more innovatively.

Core Abilities: Critical, creative, and systems thinking. The Core Abilities are imperative for learning and adapting to new situations.

Core Thinking Practices: The Practices are a way for individuals and teams to discuss simple and complex systems that shape and drive organizations. They are not meant to be followed as a process or applied as a procedure. Instead, the Practices consist of a common language and patterns, guideposts, and tools that all lead to one thing: generation of thoughtful questions. The language gives diverse teams a way to describe a situation. The patterns serve as a lens to examine typical business dynamics, enabling teams to identify causes and forecast possible outcomes. The guideposts help people avoid unwittingly contributing to the very problems that they're trying to solve. The tools surface biases and incomplete mental models that are often at the root of endless nonproductive discussions or failed efforts. The Practices trigger critical-, creative-, and systems-thinking abilities to help people think more systemically about decisions and actions.

Creative Thinking: While critical thinking uncovers pertinent data points to weigh dynamic situations, creative thinking generates potential solutions. It is an innate ability that all of us can develop.

Critical Thinking: The purpose of critical thinking is to understand a situation or problem with the ultimate goal of formulating a solution. At the core of an effective critical thinker is a person who asks good questions. Critical thinkers study a situation at the core, analyzing its makeup, cause, and the many factors involved. The output of critical thinking comprises the answers to the questions "Why?" and "How?"

Critical Thinking Tools: These tools address the perennial problems faced by organizations: synthesis of incomplete and unclear information, and awareness of deeply rooted biases and mental models. With the help of the critical-thinking tools and reflective dialogue, learners practice identifying relevant and diagnostic information from an increasing volume of ambiguous and contradictory data.

Decision Making: A Value Skill, decision making is best learned in the real-life contexts of an organization. Individuals best improve their decision-making skills in the context of real-world situations, in which they have time to reflect, evaluate, adjust, and reevaluate the impacts of their actions. People make better decisions in the workplace when they are encouraged to recognize their personal and professional biases, examine broader alternative hypotheses, and appreciate uncertainty.

Delayed Feedback: As a business acts toward a goal, the teams making the decisions are often operating under delayed feedback. If employees are not aware of the delay, unwarranted changes may be implemented because of delays in real data.

Derailers: Derailers—such as biases, lack of attention, fear, having too many choices, and dealing with a constant barrage of noise—impact thinking to such an extreme that an individual's ability to learn, much less think, is rendered dull.

Emotional Throttle: A design principle used to change team dynamics and individual engagement. By adjusting the throttle, we can influence decision making, collaboration, and a myriad of other human dynamics. For example, simply increasing the amount of information during a round tends to increase team strain and decrease the number of decisions a team makes during that round. Providing too many decision points might cause participants to resort to guessing, and providing too few might cause participants to overanalyze or become less engaged.

Fear: A derailer that impacts our ability to learn. Fear is showing up more and more at all levels in organizations and, in fact, is *the* most common source of internal noise. Fear of failure, fear of making the wrong decision, and fear of inadequacy all affect the actions people take and decisions they make.

How-to-Think Training: A systemic approach to learning. An alternative approach that recognizes the patterns and underlying structures that contribute to a system's behavior. This changes the focus from quick fixes or attributing failure to others to finding ways to improve the system.

Impact Mapping: A process to help employees at all levels see and understand the big picture. Impact mapping is derivative of causal loop diagramming and system modeling. Unless individuals and teams see the big picture and understand how the various functions or operations interconnect, their actions tend to be both self-serving and short term in their impact.

Lack of Attention: A derailer that impacts our ability to learn. With so many different things commanding our attention during a given workday, it has become increasingly difficult to focus our attention on any one thing. This constant connection to technology can actually negatively affect our productivity and effectiveness.

Leverage Point: A leverage point is a small adjustment we make within the system that changes how the system behaves. A low leverage point means a small action yields little change. A high leverage point means a small action yields a larger change in behavior throughout the system.

Limiting Beliefs: The core beliefs that we personally hold to be true are created from the fabric of our experience. The stronger those beliefs are, the harder we will work to find evidence to support them. But most of our beliefs about the world are only true because we've decided they are. Beliefs are formed through repeated thoughts, and most beliefs are formed unconsciously. Limiting beliefs are those that keep us from seeing, believing, or experiencing the true facts about something.

Mental Models: Mental models are the lenses through which we see the world and everything in it. They bring meaning to an event, fill in gaps when information is missing, and influence how we feel and react to others. Mental models represent how we see ourselves, other people, and the organization. A flawed mental model leads to misunderstandings, incorrect assumptions, and, often, poor decisions.

Microsim: A microsim generally is a shorter simulation that focuses on a few skills. It is often included in classroom activities or embedded within e-learning modules to increase the richness and provide skill practice.

Mode Analysis: An assessment technique, mode analysis investigates which parts of the brain (modes) an individual relies on most, or the personality style he exhibits during difficult situations. Modes define how we process information, communicate, relate with others, and make decisions.

Neural Coding System: Neural coding is a neuroscience-related field concerned with how sensory and other information is represented in the brain by networks of neurons. Neural coding describes the process of neural network formation in the brain in response to a stimulus. The formation of these neural networks determines how we respond to future stimuli. With repetition of any stimuli and response, neural pathways are etched deeply and become the default "programming" for how we behave or respond to similar types of stimuli. This is the neurological basis for habits and mental models. The Neural Coding System is a design framework that consists of four cognitive conditions—create optimal tension, engage mental models, activate Core Abilities, surface limiting beliefs—which, when they exist together, create an optimal learning environment for developing *how-to-think* workers.

Neural Pathways: Neural pathways are like trails through the woods. If one person walks on a path one time, the trail will barely be defined and will vanish quickly. But if many people walk the trail, there will be a defined path that is easy to see. These defined neural pathways become a comfort zone, a mental model. We tend to fit many situations into these networks, and, as a result, often we only explore options that fit our mental model. This is how habits are formed.

Neuroplasticity: The brain's ability to adapt its structural and functional organization.

Noise: The constant barrage of information and interruptions that obscure judgment and reduce the ability to think and communicate clearly. Noise presents itself in multiple ways. *World noise* is the constant onslaught of news of collapsing governments, wars, uprisings, and acts of terrorism that shape our thinking. *Organizational noise* comes in endless streams of reports, metrics, memos, slide decks, e-mails, tweets, messages, and posts. At the individual level, there is *internal noise*, which manifests from our biases, fears, and too many competing priorities.

Problem Solving: A Value Skill, problem solving is considered the most complex of all intellectual functions, a higher-order cognitive process that requires the modulation and control of more routine or fundamental skills. In fact, problem solving requires a combination of critical, systems, and creative thinking, as well as the Value Skills of decision making and collaboration.

Responsive Modeling: Responsive Modeling combines system dynamics and agent-based modeling to create an adaptive environment to challenge participants to think differently. The models respond to participant, organizational, and market inputs and outputs. Responsive Modeling has been used extensively with executive teams to develop shared mental models of how an organization works within its broader system, and to test various "what-if" scenarios. This technique has helped shape organizations of all sizes and types.

Richness and Reach Model: *Richness* is defined as the impact of the learning. *Reach* refers to the number of people who participate in the training. The higher on the Richness axis a solution falls, the greater the depth of learning is. The further to the right on the Reach axis a solution falls, the greater the number of participants is.

Self-Awareness: Unconditional positive regard means to relate to another person without judgment, to listen in a manner that causes the other person to feel heard, to accept fully what might be weaknesses of another, and to provide an open, supportive presence. While we would all welcome this quality of relationship, it is difficult to achieve because it is dependent on an individual's ability to acknowledge her own manufactured beliefs. This is done through self-awareness.

Self-Generated Insights: Real learning happens in the moment when a person combines knowledge and experiences to create something new, such as a new mental model or belief. I can tell you how a system works, but unless you experiment with it, then you're merely sharing my perspective of how I think it works. You have your own knowledge and experiences, and if you're going to be effective at making decisions within the system, then you need to construct your own perspective.

Shared or Systems Language: As the world continues to become more interconnected, having a shared language to explain dynamic situations will be essential for people of diverse backgrounds and cultures to work together to solve problems. This is why systems language is so powerful. The language provides a way for people of varying backgrounds to discuss and explore systems.

SimGate: SimGate is proprietary software used to design, develop, and deliver training in all four quadrants of the Richness and Reach diagram. Its primary capabilities are optimized for developing the *how-to-think* skills and abilities.

Simulation: Simulations offer experiential learning and are targeted at global organizations requiring deep learning and global reach. These simulations incorporate the tools necessary for teams to collaborate in solving complex problems.

System Dynamics: An approach to understanding the behavior of complex systems by taking into consideration interconnected parts, feedback loops, and delays.

Systems Thinking: The concept of systems thinking is a way of seeing the world as a confluence of systems—all systems that influence our daily lives, our organizations, and, ultimately, our actions. Systems thinking provides a way to view situations or problems within the context of the larger systems that created them, creating a framework for critical and creative thinking to produce true insights. Systems thinkers look at cause and effect, relationships, feedback, delays, and unintended consequences to find a balance point.

The Thinking Effect: A cycle of improving our thinking, applying it to any situation, and learning from the outcome; an experience that changes our mental models. The Thinking Effect is both an individual experience and a collective process an organization can jumpstart for its employees. The most powerful aspect of the Thinking Effect is that everyone can learn to participate in it.

U-Shaped Learning: U-shaped learning is the typical pattern by which many physical, artistic, and cognitive skills are developed. Skills developed in the "U-shaped" fashion begin on a high performance level and over time the skills descend to a lower performance level. After time, the skill once again ascends to a higher level. The pattern creates a U-shaped curve when graphed.

Value Continuum Model: This is a mental model used to examine the phases that exceptional thinkers and doers go through in their careers. In this book, it is shown as a graph that depicts the ratio of value produced by an employee to the costs of employing him.

Value Skills: The skills of decision making, problem solving, and collaborating are defined as Value Skills. Ultimately, the Value Skills define an individual's value potential.

Value Worker: A Value Worker is an individual who has developed the ability to make better decisions and solve problems collaboratively in dynamic and complex situations. This person is equipped to unlearn and relearn quickly as she encounters new and changing situations.

What-to-Think Training: A linear approach to learning that involves traditional training programs, which are designed to improve performance in a specific area of practice. Most produce training that focuses on the bottom three levels of Bloom's Taxonomy: Knowledge, Comprehension, and Application. *What-to-think* training has a real purpose. It provides consistency and a common way of thinking. Understanding processes, methodologies, and the organizational "way" is imperative to preparing employees.

WorkTank: WorkTanks combine learning and the actual production of needed work product for the organization. For example, within a strategic alignment WorkTank, participants develop actual strategies and vet them by running various scenarios across different market conditions.

Bibliography

Amabile, Teresa, Constance N. Hadley, and Steven J. Kramer. "Creativity Under the Gun." *Harvard Business Review* Vol. 80, No. 8, August 2002.

Andrew, Jim, Joe Manget, David Michael, Andrew Taylor, and Hadi Zablit. "Innovation 2010: A Return to Prominence and the Emergence of a New World Order." The Boston Consulting Group, April 2010.

Argyris, Chris. *Overcoming Organizational Defenses*. Upper Saddle River, NJ: Prentice Hall, 1990.

Arum, Richard, and Josipa Roksa. *Academically Adrift: Limited Learning on College Campuses*. Chicago: University of Chicago Press, 2011.

Begley, Sharon. "I Can't Think." *Newsweek Magazine*, Brain Freeze, March 2011.

Benson, Joy, and Sally Dresdow. "Discovery Mindset: A Decision-Making Model for Discovery and Collaboration." *Management Decision*, Vol. 41, No. 10, 2003.

Bloom, Benjamin. *Taxonomy of Educational Objectives*. Boston: Allyn and Bacon, 1956.

Brookfield, Stephen. *Training Educators of Adults: The Theory and Practice of Graduate Adult Education*. New York: Routledge, 1988.

Camp, Paul J. "U-Shaped Development of Newtonian Concepts: Implications for Pedagogical Design and Research Practice." Atlanta: Georgia Tech, 2012.

Cappelli, Peter. *Talent on Demand: Managing Talent in an Age of Uncertainty*. Boston: Harvard Business School Press, 2008.

Coyle, Daniel. *The Talent Code*. New York: Bantam Dell, 2009.

Cyert, Richard, and James G. March. *A Behavioral Theory of the Firm*. Upper Saddle River, NJ: Prentice-Hall, 1963.

Dimoka, Angelika. Center for Neural Decision Making, Fox School of Business, Temple University, http://www.fox.temple.edu/minisites/neural/index.html.

Dörner, Dietrich. *The Logic of Failure: Recognizing and Avoiding Error in Complex Situations*. New York: Metropolitan Books, 1996.

Drucker, Peter. *The Effective Executive*. New York: Harper & Row, 1967.

Fisher, Lawrence M. "The Prophet of Unintended Consequences." *Strategy+Business*, Fall 2005, issue 40.

Fisher, Robert. "Creative Minds: Building Communities of Learning for the Creative Age." Paper presented at the Teaching Qualities Initiative international conference, Hong Kong, 2002. www.teachingthinking.net.

Fiske, Susan T., and Shelley E. Taylor. *Social Cognition*. New York: McGraw-Hill Higher Education, 2007.

Forrester, Jay W. *World Dynamics*. Cambridge, MA: Wright-Allen Press, 1971.

Frank, Loren. University of California at San Francisco, the Frank Laboratory at UCSF, http://www.keck.ucsf.edu/~loren/.

Gardner, Howard. *Frames of Mind: The Theory of Multiple Intelligences*. New York: Basic Books, 1983.

Glassman, James K. "Dihydrogen Monoxide: Unrecognized Killer." *The Orlando Sentinel*, October 28, 1997.

Goodman, Michael. Innovation Associates Organizational Learning. http://innovationassociates.com.

Harris, Robert. "Introduction to Creative Thinking," July 1, 1998, www.virtualsalt.com.

Hay Group. http://www.haygroup.com.

Henry, James. *In a Fisherman's Language*. Pawcatuck, CT: Fisherman's Language, LLC, 2012.

IBM Global Business Services. *Capitalizing on Complexity: Insights from the Global Chief Executive Officer Study*. Somers, NY: IBM Global Business Services, 2010.

iSee Systems, http://www.iseesystems.com/Online_Training/course/
module1/1-04-0-0-where.htm.

Kahneman, Daniel. *Thinking, Fast and Slow*. New York: Farrar, Straus &
Giroux, 2011.

Kegan, Robert, and Lisa Laskow Lahey. "The Real Reason People Won't
Change." *Harvard Business Review*, November 2001.

Kembel, George. "The Classroom in 2020." *Forbes*, April 8, 2010.

Lovallo, Dan, and Oliver Sibony. "The Case for Behavioral Strategy."
McKinsey Quarterly, March 2010.

Mark, Gloria, Victor M. Gonzalez, and Justin Harris. "No Task Left Behind?
Examining the Nature of Fragmented Work." *Proceedings of the 2005
Conference on Human Factors in Computing Systems*, CHI 2005, Port-
land, Oregon, April 2–7, 2005.

Miller, George A. "The Magical Number Seven, Plus or Minus Two: Some
Limits on Our Capacity for Processing Information." *The Psychological Review*, 1956.

"Neuroplasticity and the Brain." www.transforming-child-behavior.com/
neuroplasticity.html.

Patoine, Brenda. "Applying Insights from the Study of Normal Aging to
Solve Dementia." *2009 Advances in Brain Research*, The Dana Foundation, 2009.

Paul, Richard W., and Linda Elder. *Critical Thinking: Tools for Taking Charge
of Your Professional and Personal Life*. Upper Saddle River, NJ: Pearson
Education, 2002.

Petrie, Nicholas. "Future Trends in Leadership Development," White-
paper, Center for Creative Leadership, January 2012.

Pfeffer, Jeffrey, and Robert I. Sutton. *The Knowing-Doing Gap: How Smart
Companies Turn Knowledge into Action*. Boston: Harvard Business
School Press, 2000.

Poldrack, Russell. "Multi-Tasking Adversely Affects the Brain's Learning
Systems." UCLA Department of Psychology, July 26, 2006.

Richtel, Matt. "Your Brain on Computers: Digital Devices Deprive Brain
of Needed Downtime." *New York Times*, April 25, 2010.

Rock, David, and Jeffrey Schwartz. "The Neuroscience of Leadership."
      Strategy & Leadership, Vol. 43, May 2006.

Rogers, Carl. *On Becoming a Person*. New York: Houghton Mifflin, 1961.

Schmid, Randolf E. "Study Finds People Who Multitask Often Bad At It."
      US News and World Report, August 24, 2009.

Schwartz, Barry. *The Paradox of Choice: Why More Is Less*. New York: Harp-
      erCollins, 2004.

Senge, Peter. *The Fifth Discipline: The Art and Practice of the Learning Orga-
      nization*. New York: Doubleday/Currency, 1990.

Sterman, John D. *Business Dynamics: Systems Thinking and Modeling for a
      Complex World*. Burr Ridge, IL: McGraw-Hill Higher Education, 2000.

The Millennium Project. "15 Global Challenges Facing Humanity." Last
      modified in 2009, www.millennium-project.org/millennium/
      challeng.html.

The Millennium Project. "State of the Future Report." www.millennium-
      project.org/millennium/2012SOF.html.

Thompson, Clive. "Meet the Life Hackers." *The New York Times Magazine*,
      October 16, 2005.

Van DeMille, Oliver. *A Thomas Jefferson Education: Teaching a Generation
      of Leaders for the Twenty-First Century*. Cedar City, UT: George Wythe
      College Press, 2002.

Vohs, Kathleen D., Roy F. Baumeister, Brandon J. Schmeichel, Jean M.
      Twenge, Noelle M. Nelson, and Dianne M. Tice. "Making Choices
      Impairs Subsequent Self-Control: A Limited-Resource Account of
      Decision Making, Self-Regulation, and Active Initiative." *Journal of
      Personality and Social Psychology*, Vol. 94, No. 5, 2008.

Vonnegut, Kurt. "Harrison Bergeron." *The Magazine of Fantasy and Sci-
      ence Fiction*. Mercury Publications, October 1961.

Walker, Rod. Systems modeler. Altus Consulting, Inc.

Whorf, Benjamin Lee. "Science and Linguistics." *MIT's Technology
      Review*, April 1940.

Wikipedia. Donald O. Hebb. http://en.wikipedia.org/wiki/
      Donald_O._Hebb.

Index

· ·

Index